The LIBERATION *of* THOUGHT

GARY BRYANT

BALBOA.
PRESS
A DIVISION OF HAY HOUSE

Balboa Press books may be ordered through booksellers or by contacting:

Balboa Press
A Division of Hay House
1663 Liberty Drive
Bloomington, IN 47403
www.balboapress.com
1 (877) 407-4847

Because of the dynamic nature of the Internet, any web addresses or links contained in this book may have changed since publication and may no longer be valid. The views expressed in this work are solely those of the author and do not necessarily reflect the views of the publisher, and the publisher hereby disclaims any responsibility for them.

The author of this book does not dispense medical advice or prescribe the use of any technique as a form of treatment for physical, emotional, or medical problems without the advice of a physician, either directly or indirectly. The intent of the author is only to offer information of a general nature to help you in your quest for emotional and spiritual well-being. In the event you use any of the information in this book for yourself, which is your constitutional right, the author and the publisher assume no responsibility for your actions.

Any people depicted in stock imagery provided by Thinkstock are models, and such images are being used for illustrative purposes only. Certain stock imagery © Thinkstock.

ISBN: 978-1-5043-4543-9 (sc)
ISBN: 978-1-5043-4544-6 (e)

Print information available on the last page.

Balboa Press rev. date: 11/16/2015

TABLE OF CONTENTS

PREFACE

The serious author wishes to reach and in some way benefit readers while simultaneously advancing his own discovery and development. Thus an author worthy of the name writes in order to further his being, and the craft of writing is properly placed as one among many ways to actualize the life to which he aspires.

A similar consideration obtains in the communication of a serious thinker, and no topic is more serious or weighty than the idea of thought itself. It is perhaps tempting to label a thinker a philosopher, but not all who think well are philosophers, though, of course, many are. Yet the assumption that we are already prepared for and well suited to serious thought is rarely questioned, and consequently many thinkers have not approached this question until a considerable amount of thought or reason has already been expended.

When a given thinker begins to question this assumption, what is often disclosed by further thought is that thought, or reason, is actually in service to something else in the human structure, and this "something else" is usually said to be passion, or desire. Having reached this conclusion, the thinker either casts about for some remedy to this unforeseen development, or resigns himself to it, thereby casting a shadow of doubt upon the objectivity of thought itself.

Those who seek for a remedy must begin to question, not the conclusion itself, but the state of being to which it points. If thought is indeed enslaved by passion, then just how much credence can we place upon any conclusions reached by such thought – including the conclusion that thought is enslaved. Or could it be that our inquiry would better be served by examining not thought, but passion? What is the nature of passion, or desire, and what is it about this feature of the human being that allows it to subvert the putative objectivity of thought, to call into question thought's claim to be the ruling faculty of human nature?

In the history of thought, East and West, these two tributaries, remedy and resignation, tend to dominate the response to thought's apparent servitude to passion. By and large, Eastern thought tends toward remedy, while Western thought tends toward resignation. To be sure, there is an exception here and there, both East and West, but such exceptions highlight the rule. In the East, remedies are approached by first inquiring into the fundamental existential quandary in which human beings begin to examine not only their separate faculties but also their overall identities. In the West, resignation usually issues in a series of reevaluations of the scope and limitations of what is commonly dubbed "reason." In both East and West, thought or reason as conventionally conceived is severely chastened, either through a sought after remedy or through a resigned reformulation.

Both approaches, remedy and resignation, correctly critique thought as conventionally conceived, and thereby call for a revaluation of values, an inquiry into not only the nature of thought and passion but also of human identity. Both approaches seek to come to terms with what appears to be a universally recognized human condition: the enslavement of what at first blush presents itself as the only rational alternative to the utterly chaotic nature of human desires – thought or reason.

Another universal expression of human concern, East and West, is the question of being and becoming, often formulated as a concern for both certainty, as a quality of being, and development, as a quality of becoming. In Western modes of thought, particular individuals have either tried to reconcile certainty and development in their own thought, or have emphasized one to the detriment of the other. Yet the universal concern of both being and becoming, certainty and development, continues to bedevil thought, partly because it too touches upon the question of thought itself.

What part does being play in thought's enslavement to desire, and what part does becoming play? Until these questions are investigated, how can we determine certainty at all? And how does development enter into both remedy and resignation? To seek a remedy is to search for a way to free thought from passion; in such a case, development must lead from uncertainty to certainty. Yet how can a process of becoming lead to a state of being? And how can a state of being like thought's servitude issue in a developmental process from enslavement to liberation?

Because of the unhappy conclusion regarding thought's servitude to passion, it is difficult to see how thinking itself can remedy the situation. Certainly thought enslaved by desire cannot do so. Is there another thought possible, another quality of thought not so enslaved? A higher thought, perhaps, that can critique ordinary thought in service to a higher, more refined desire? For it is, after all, passion or desire as a state of being that must be investigated, and without some access to a more elevated thought such inquiry must founder upon the inability of ordinary reason or *ratio* to liberate itself.

Liberated thought points beyond itself to the reality that informs it. The finest Eastern thought, for example, is characterized by an evocation of an intelligence beyond words or concepts; words are used to woo us *from* words. If concepts are to be used at all, they must serve to undermine the conceptual mind. Liberated thought must be sly.

Such is the inquiry that motivates the author of this book, and insofar as this question calls to the reader he, or she, is invited to join the author in his quest. For the universal concerns outlined in this preface also issue inevitably in the equally universal concern of identity, a concern that can only be engaged with a Thought free enough to be capable of the most sincere and difficult self-inquiry.

CHAPTER ONE

THOUGHT AND DESIRE

Ordinary Thought

Ordinary thought takes several forms: associative thought, attracted thought, and directed thought. Associative thinking is the most automatic, one idea associated with another and in turn with yet another to form a chain of associations, typically with little or no direction or aim. Attracted thought contains an element of emotion, a chain of reasoning initiated by an attraction to a particular idea or topic. Directed thought is the most difficult and demands a measure of attention to reasoning: working out a problem, writing a coherent essay, learning a craft, and so on.

Associative thought is like one wandering aimlessly; attracted thought is like one driven by a desire to attain a predisposed destination; directed thought is like one driven by desire to remain on a predisposed path despite repeated inclinations to wander onto side roads; authentic thought, which must be distinguished from the forms of thought already mentioned, is like one submitting to the direction of a guide, free of the desire to travel a predetermined path to a predisposed location, open to take unknown paths and explore unknown regions.

Ordinary thought is a function of the disconnected intellect, and the primary reason such thought is usually considered the highest form of thought and so the acme of rationality is that the intellect or mind is considered to be the only instrument of knowing, the only center of intelligence, in the human being. What is missing in this belief, and what authentic spiritual schools understand, is the recognition of several other "brains" or centers of intelligence besides the isolated head brain: several lower centers and two higher centers. The lower centers include those associated with the somatic structure, such as the instinctive, sexual, and moving centers, and the feeling or emotional center. The two higher centers are the higher emotional and higher intellect.

Acquaintance with these additional centers of knowing is confined to initiates in authentic spiritual schools, several of which will be examined in subsequent chapters. For now, it is enough to know that without such an initiation the usual conclusion drawn by the isolated intellect, the head brain, is that the quality of thought with which it is familiar is the only rationality possible, and the study of thought is confined to the study of that sort of reasoning.

Philosophical Thought

In the West particularly, but also in parts of the East influenced by the West, philosophical thought is considered the acme of rationality. This sort of thought usually addresses questions relating to the nature of reality or being, the scope and limits of knowledge – that is, how can we know reality – and what ought we do in interacting with rational beings like ourselves.

In all three areas – ontology, epistemology, and deontology – a measure of certainty about the content of our thought is sought. A perfect rationality would be certainty about the nature of the real, how it is we are able to know or be certain about the nature of the real, and an equal certainty regarding how to interact with other rational beings. In ancient Western spiritual or philosophical schools, the attainment of certainty was dependent upon a development of being, in particular a development of the lower emotional center that would attract the descent of the energy of the higher emotional center. Later philosophical thought, not privy to this understanding, tried futilely to attain certainty using the unaided and disconnected rationality of the isolated intellect.

The subsequent development of this unaided rationality led inexorably to resignation about what "pure" reason could know: the conclusion was that reason could not know the real at all; all it could know was how the real must appear to us, shaped decisively by the categories of our "understanding." And yet another kind of thought, scientific thought, was teaching just the opposite: that we could be certain about our knowledge.

Scientific Thought

During the same period that philosophical thought in the West was reaching its resignation regarding what we can know, scientific thought declared that we have certain knowledge about reality using the theoretical protocols of Newtonian physics. David Hume, coming at the end of a line of British empiricists, maintained that this belief was based upon an illusion, the mistaken idea that the scientific notion of cause and effect is actually capable of being observed. Hume argued that all our knowledge comes via the senses, what we observe, and at no time do we ever observe one thing causing another. The underpinnings of science, the putative certainty of scientific knowledge, rests upon a mistaken belief.

Immanuel Kant was convinced that the Newtonian theoretical account of the world and its laws was indeed certain, and was disturbed that philosophical thought appeared to be undermining that certainty. Yet if we can't locate the certainty we feel in our observation of the world, where can it be found? Kant hit upon the idea that the certainty is in how our minds must impose their categories of understanding – like cause and effect – upon whatever the real may be, and through such imposition are able to conceive and thus perceive things in the only way possible for us.

A brilliant "solution" certainly, but one which has also imposed a dark shroud of uncertainty upon any attempt to pierce the world of appearance to the nature of reality itself, and one which has ever since consigned Western thought to resignation about the limitations of reason. Ordinary thought, even the most clever and ingenious, can never penetrate the veil of appearance, can never know the real. Thus the reason of the disconnected, unaided intellect is severely chastened – and rightly so: it is a travesty of authentic rationality.

Reason and Desire

Another conclusion which Hume reached is that reason is the slave of the passions, a truth well known in ancient Western philosophical schools. Hume reached this conclusion based upon ordinary observation, yet a deeper and broader understanding must include how the process of desire itself enlists *ratio* or the reason of the isolated intellect through the creation and continuing reinforcement of a mistaken identity or sense of self.

The *process* of desire is a process of identification, a dynamic understood by all authentic spiritual schools and their teachings. An impulse to meet a given need is naturally released in the human structure, and during this process the energy or feeling of one's self, one's identity, is identified with the impulse that in turn creates a specific desire; this desire is usually a distant and distorted echo of the originating need, and in meeting the desire the need is not met.

The best example of how a need is unmet due to the process of desire is the need for Being. The need for Being is a need to develop an intermediate level of being or feeling, midway between the mistaken sense of selfhood created by family and society and the authentic Identity or Self. This development is needed in order to transition from a mistaken identity to the true Identity. But the need goes unmet as the process of desire or identification creates a distant echo of that need with a specific desire both expressive and reinforcing of an already mistaken sense of self or identity. Typical desires that are at best distorted expressions of the need for Being include various addictions and compulsions, desires that appear endless in their ever-receding incapacity to satisfy because of the infinite nature of their true object: Being itself.

A Free Thought

In order for thought to be free, liberated, the process of desire must be understood not only intellectually but also emotionally and somatically, with all the lower centers of intelligence, harmonized and united by higher emotional energy. And for that to occur the different levels and qualities of attention must be understood, felt, and sensed.

The lowest level or quality of attention is the attention associated with the disconnected mind or head brain. Its level is usually too low and passive to be a force of awakening; it therefore forms part of the soporific state that obtains in human beings most of the time. At the same time, it is also that sort of attention with which we are most familiar, the attention that we can place on this or that object of desire, for example, or simply choose to single out one object over others with one or more of our senses. We see in this ability to focus or direct our attention an element of choice or freedom, provided we study its working. And during this study we observe a certain ability of our attention to elevate itself, to become more active, finer in quality.

A more active attention makes possible a kind of observation of ourselves, a kind of mind-observation, in which we perceive an attention in the other lower brains, an attention of feeling and of the somatic structure, the body and its functions. This observation also reveals an inclination for each attention to go its own way, heedless of the others, captivated by its own desires, often conflicting desires. The head may want to lose weight, while the body wants to eat another piece of pie, and the feeling may be indifferent, occupied with another desire entirely. This typical scenario reveals our usual, fragmented state of being, and absent any sort of observation these attentions are not even aware of their disconnection with the others. Yet in fact each attention shares with the others the illusion of a false identity, a socially constructed sense of self that acts as a partition screening off each attention from the others and preventing each from recognizing the fragmented condition of the whole. The illusion is that there is an authentic self that provides unity and continuity; the reality is that only fragmentation and discontinuity obtain in the human structure.

In the right conditions, in school conditions, an interest, caused by observation of this fragmentation, begins to grow, a certain feeling of remorse, a feeling that another possibility of being human is available, one that promises unity and continuity as a fact of being rather than the fiction it has proven to be. But for this possibility to be actualized help is needed. One can discover the fact of fragmentation, but one is helpless to unify the disparate parts. At the same time, however, it is possible to receive the needed help with a more active attention, an attention that can elevate itself and in so doing correspond in quality and fineness to the even finer energy or feeling needed to begin the process of alchemical transformation, the process of harmonizing and so unifying the lower brains or centers.

Higher Attention, Higher Thought

We have seen how attention can be elevated enough to observe the functions of the lower brains, including the head brain. And the primary function of the head brain is thought, which we have also examined: the different forms of ordinary thought. An even higher attention is beyond this sort of thought, and is in fact a higher thought.

Creative individuals often speak of their most treasured ideas or thoughts as insights that have come to them in an entirely different way than even directed thought with its attention to reasoning. Sometimes they speak of such insights as though they are inspirations or revelations from another level of being altogether. Such an insight is not an idea arrived at by a train of reasoning, and it seems to be a higher level of seeing penetrating into the more usual, ordinary thought process. It is something of a mystery.

Authentic thought is the penetration of a higher level of awareness into a lower level, and the highest level of thought is a seeing without concepts, beyond concepts. And in the development of being, upon which the development of thought depends, the attachment of thought to concepts is the most difficult impediment to the understanding of real thought, of real seeing. In all spiritual traditions and schools the conceptual mind, the content of thought, is the fundamental factor undergirding the ersatz sense of self. For that reason the first order of business is to disengage the formidable association of the conceptual mind with authentic thought or seeing.

That seeing, real thought, is senior to the conceptual mind becomes more and more obvious as mind-observation becomes more and more familiar. Whatever the content of the mind, whatever the concepts or ideas, seeing comprehends such content with a more comprehensive vision, a seeing of what is. This vision is insight, Thought or Attention, an awareness of what is the case.

Awareness of Desire

Once the disengagement of Thought from the conceptual mind obtains, attention can find itself senior to the entire process of desire as the content of ordinary thought begins to lose its authority and attention naturally becomes more active, no longer passive before a bogus self-sense with its conceptual conceits.

The study of the process of desire in turn yields an understanding of different qualities of desire. Some desires are faithful reflections of real need, the best example being the desire for greater Being, the ontological desire. Others, the vast majority given the usual authority of a mistaken identity, are distant and distorted reflections of real need, so distant that the need is unmet even as the desire is satisfied.

The ontological desire, reflecting the need for Being, is a call to open to and receive a higher level of Thought, of Awareness, that is itself Being, and that can initiate a process of development in the human structure, a development of intermediate being. The more this development obtains, the more Being can be received, and the more Being received, the more development occurs. Thus Being, and the certainty vouchsafed by Being, and development, or becoming, work together in providing the needed help to individuals called to actualize the possibility of authentic human unity and continuity.

The Need for School Conditions

One need that is so often not met even among those galvanized by an inner search for Being is the need for the developmental conditions only provided by an authentic school of inner work. For one of the chief conceits of the disconnected, unsubmitted mind is that a course of inner growth can be conducted alone.

The difficulty in challenging such a conceit is that it forms an inseparable part of the overall sense of self inculcated by society and all its institutions, the foundational one being one's family of origin. Particularly in the United States, individualism is touted to such a degree that each one is convinced that it is possible to attain any worthwhile objective alone – with a measure of assistance along the way, but by and large alone. This conceit is carried over to the spiritual, inner life, and can lead to all manner of spiritual delusions and fantasies, the worst of which is the conviction that an intellectual understanding of an inner teaching constitutes an enlightened or liberated state of being. Because of the dangers involved in such a fantasy, well established school conditions are needed to contain egoic delusions and provide the needed support for an initial phase of shock and awe.

The shock comes as the conventionally minded individual is invited to use his attention for something other than to pursue an egoic desire; when self-observation begins to develop, one is shocked to discover that one is not at all who one imagines, and neither can one do what one imagines. The awe comes as the first sort of shock yields to the shock of awakening, a discovery of who one really is and what one can really do. Such discoveries initiate the slower and more difficult process of inner development, and here too one needs the support of a community or school: the guidance of elders who have been through the experiences one is currently enduring, and the fellowship of others who are undergoing their own shocks.

What prevents utter bewilderment and despair at these usually unwelcome revelations is the ongoing opportunity to ask for the guidance of elders in a given school. One is taught that the search for Being is an ongoing process of questioning, and that during regular meetings with peers and elders one has the opportunity to put questions and to receive, not answers, but responses that deepen one's questions and so advance the search for the Being that will meet one's ontological need. And what prevents a feeling of isolation and abandonment is the fellow-feeling that develops among those who are at the same level of understanding in the school, the mutual support that eventually issues in a strong feeling of community, of a communal house of work.

Serious and effective inner work, then, is not for the faint of heart, neither is it for the loner: it demands individual courage to face one's truth along with a willingness to submit to the guidance of elders and the necessary rules and boundaries of the school itself. In addition, authentic spiritual work is fraught with danger, and in some cases of spiritual emergence, or emergency, a community or school with protective safeguards is essential; without it, an individual can easily lose the way, his self, and even his sanity. To give only one example, serious questioning of the conventional self-sense demands a stable enough sense of self to endure such interrogation. The sort of exposure to the truth characteristic of an authentic spiritual school is not the place for anyone with a shaky or dissociated self-sense, and precautions are taken by elders to prevent such a one from entering that demanding path.

School conditions are also required to woo an individual, particularly one with a clever mind, from a reliance upon the conceptual mind with its psychological and logical orientation to a reliance upon the higher mind with its energetic orientation, beyond conceptual thought. The mistaken notion that conceptual thought can be objectively true must be thoroughly discredited. This task can be aided by some conclusions of secular thought, for example the Western conclusion that reason cannot know the real. Yet by and large this reorientation of an individual from psychology to energy is a formidable enterprise, and many who enter serious school conditions are still unable to make the transition. To make this transition one must shift attention from the isolated intellect to the body and, above all, to feeling.

It is like learning a language: one can attempt to master a language with course work and audio material, but there is no substitute for immersing oneself in a country where the language is spoken, preferably for a few years. Similarly, there is no substitute for immersing oneself in school conditions for many years if one ever hopes to become more interested in currents of somatic energy and feeling than in a lifetime of interest in conceptual thought. The conditioning of parents, peers, and the holding culture is simply too daunting otherwise.

The Transition to Energy

With the question of an energetic orientation we come upon the most difficult hurdle in understanding Thought in its pure form as a seeing beyond conceptual thought, as a comprehensive vision of what is. For the reception of higher Thought or Seeing is not a disembodied state: it is the reception of the Force or Energy needed to see objectively, a force received in the somatic tissues of the body.

This needed participation of the body has been all but forgotten in current spiritual circles, and no spiritual school can be considered authentic without an understanding of this reception. The energy of the higher mind is the active force, and the body, properly prepared by school conditions, is the passive or receptive force. Together these two forces call the feeling – not the ersatz feeling of egoic emotion, but the finer feeling of Being, corresponding to the higher emotional center. Both shock and awe inform this feeling, and a door is opened for the descent of an energetic current, the life-force, that can initiate alchemical transformation in the body. And it is for the sake of this transformation that a transition of interest to the energetic is needed.

During this transition two developments occur: one is the introduction to authentic Thought, vision, or seeing; the other is the liberation of ordinary thought. Authentic Thought is an energetic, embodied seeing; liberated, ordinary thought more and more closely approaches what spiritual schools call pondering, the frequent returning to a question that one holds before the mind and about which one entertains an ongoing reflection. Thought that has been freed from the desiring process is also free to ponder the most serious and fateful questions of human existence. And the most fateful question of all is that of identity: who am I?

Paradigmatic Pondering

Pondering is a paradigm of liberated thought. It is a form of thought informed by higher vision and free of the desire to obtain a particular outcome or result. And as one gains experience in pondering one begins to see how most thought is driven by desire.

Pondering cannot be truly engaged so long as one trusts in the authority of conceptual thought. For conceptual thought, ordinary reason or rationality, seduces us into believing that it can deliver truth, can provide understanding of what is, of the real. Yet even such reason itself issues in a decisive refutation of that belief: both Western and Eastern thinkers of any substance have come to negative conclusions about the authority of this sort of rationality, and no longer trust in its claims to deliver the truth. What, then, is so seductive about this claim?

The seductive element is in the *desire* to know the truth, to understand reality, and it is this desire that motivates us to turn to the most readily available tool to fulfill our wish to know, the reason of the isolated head brain. And because of our fragmented condition, and the familiar yet incomplete sense of identity, we believe that the conceptual mind is the only possible rationality. Thus the desire of which I write is not the original wish to know or understand reality, but rather a distant and distorted echo of that wish, one supercharged with the misplaced energy of Being, and carrying in its train an imperative to demand of the conceptual mind what it can never deliver. Truth can never be conceptualized, neither can it be communicated conceptually.

Concepts and Sacred Ideas

Philosopher Jacob Needleman has suggested an interesting contrast in approaching the difficult notion of the conceptual mind and its claim to attain truth. This contrast is between concepts and sacred ideas.

Concepts are those ideas used by the intellect to organize experience conceptually, what one can do with ideas to advance knowledge in science and scholarship, for example. A Kantian understanding of this process would naturally acknowledge a considerable contribution of the human categories of understanding in shaping experience in the only way we can comprehend it conceptually. And with this understanding we can readily admit that our concepts cannot disclose the nature of the real but only how the real necessarily appears to us.

Sacred ideas are those ideas that serve as a catalyst to begin the long and difficult process of inner development, the mutual working of being and becoming, certainty and development, and also serve as a counterintuitive force, one of many "skillful means" intended to weaken the authority of the conceptual mind and introduce the authority of the higher mind. They are meant to call our attention to our fragmented condition and point us toward the possibility of an authentic unity and continuity. Yet the conditioning of the conceptual mind, and its putative authority, is so strong that many even in spiritual schools treat sacred ideas as concepts and rely on the conceptual mind to light the way.

For this reason one can find "fundamentalists" even in authentic schools of inner work. For them a given text, perhaps written by the founder of the school or by other authorities in that tradition of work, is treated as holy writ, verbally inspired, and consulted as an authority regarding the deeper meaning of the work of the school. Of course this approach relies upon a hermeneutical reading, both exegetical and eisegetical, with all the subjective uncertainties that obtain in interpreting textual material. A clever mind can be immersed in perpetuity in such a quagmire.

A correct approach to such material cannot be hermeneutical. For a hermeneutical approach is a conceptual approach, and the purpose of sacred ideas, sometimes contained in textual material, is to wean us from the conceptual mind and its supposed cleverness. Such material, and the sacred ideas contained therein, points beyond itself to the possible unity and continuity which alone can yield the needed understanding of Being that one can properly call truth. Such ideas point beyond the rationality of the conceptual mind to authentic rationality.

Authentic Rationality

Authentic rationality is a function of an actualized microcosm, the human being who has become, by dint of inner work, a true reflection of the cosmos. Such a one has developed sufficient being to be able to receive objective knowledge, a direct understanding of Being, of the real, of truth. The fundamental Energy of reality circulates through one's being; one understands through "standing under" higher Thought, higher Seeing.

Thus a direct knowledge of truth is possible, in direct opposition to the conclusions of the usual, ordinary rationality. The reason of the isolated intellect wrongly concludes that we must resign ourselves to inferential truth, that a direct apprehension of the real is not possible. No better example of how the process of desire blinds us to the truth exists. Because of the desiring process, our wish for Being and truth is distorted into an impatient drive to believe in reason's impudent claim to be our ruling faculty and so overlook our more fundamental existential predicament.

If we can feel the need to return to a more authentic wish or desire for knowledge, for the truth, we will need to examine the most immediate inner realities. And for this examination a school of inner work is indispensable.

CHAPTER TWO

ANCIENT WESTERN THOUGHT

The Pre-Socratics

We only have a few fragments of the writings of the pre-Socratic thinkers, those who recorded their thoughts before the dramatic and world-changing event of Socrates. From Parmenides we have speculations about being, and from Heraclitus speculations about becoming. In pre-Socratic thought, then, we have investigations into the nature of reality, and, as a part of that reality, the nature of the human being. And from the beginning both being and becoming figure importantly in this early Greek thinking.

Aside from the content of pre-Socratic thought, we also have indications about the early conditions within which this thought developed. Here, particularly in the accounts of the school of Pythagoras, we find described the organized life created to support and facilitate the development of reflections about reality. What presents itself in these accounts are descriptions of school conditions designed to assist not only the development of thought but also, and more importantly, the development of the human being. Communal forms such as the study of music, mathematics, dance and movement are mentioned, as well as shared meals and the pondering together of questions such as the nature of being.

One of the most unhelpful conclusions to be drawn about pre-Socratic thought, then, is that it is intended primarily to reach correct conclusions about reality. To miss its primordial concern is to miss the heart of all subsequent Western thought, and also to overlook the fundamental principle of communal pondering that characterizes ancient thought in the Western world. For the ultimate concern of pre-Socratic thought is the transformation of the human being; the knowledge aimed at is not the sort of knowing that characterizes modern and postmodern forms of thought, correct conclusions drawn based upon scholarly or scientific research, for example. Instead, it is a kind of knowing to which Socrates famously alludes in his insistence that he knows that he knows nothing; it is a knowing that is Being itself. Doctrines of Pythagoras or Parmenides about the nature of reality are not intended to quench the search for the knowledge of Being: on the contrary. They are intended to deepen this search, and to ignite further questioning into the mystery not only of Being but also of being human.

The Socratic Event

The advent of Socrates upon the world stage is widely considered a monumental event, for with this single individual we have a dramatic account of what it must have been like to enter into a communal search for truth in the sense not of knowing the truth but of being the truth. And it is primarily within the dialogues of Plato that we can experience a taste of this search.

Unfortunately, later Western thought has too often interpreted Socrates and his pupil Plato as rationalists, teaching the supremacy of the ordinary mind or *ratio* over the human structure. This interpretation is a complete misunderstanding of the Socratic and Platonic teaching, for their common purpose was just the opposite: their intent was to challenge and upend just that putative supremacy.

Both Socrates and Plato knew that what is most fragile in the history of serious thought is its primordial purpose: the transformation or development of the human being. And this element is most fragile because what tends to be forgotten or lost is the absolutely indispensable teaching that without school conditions the human feature that most impedes the discovery and development of the higher mind is overlooked in favor of the content of thought, of correct opinions or speculations about this or that dimension of reality. What is this feature?

The Question of Desire

"All men by nature desire to know," wrote Aristotle. Modern philosophers believe that the word of interest in this saying is *know*, whereas the real interest should be in the word *desire*. Before the question of knowledge can be properly addressed the question of desire must first be explored and pondered.

Socrates challenged the unquestioned desire for knowledge by highlighting two sorts of knowledge: the first, authentic knowledge, the knowledge of *Being*, and the second, inauthentic knowledge, the putative knowledge of *beings*, or objects, the former, direct, certain, and immediate, the latter, indirect, uncertain, and mediate, inferential. The latter Socrates termed *opinion*. All subsequent problems in determining how we know and how we can be certain stem from not only trying to elevate the uncertain "knowledge" of beings or objects to the status of real knowledge but also from the forgetfulness of Being.

"What is Being?" Another question Aristotle posed. He sought to answer this unanswerable question by appealing to different sorts of causation: material, effective, formal, and final. In so doing, he set an unfortunate precedent for Western thought: the use of reason, enslaved by the desire to know beings or objects at a distance, to "know" or discover what it cannot possibly know through the uncertain "knowledge" of beings: Being itself.

What Aristotle failed to do, at least in the lecture notes that have come down to us, was ask the anterior question alluded to by Socrates and Plato: what is desire? What is the nature of this desire to know Being? How does it become distorted into the desire to know beings? And how is the original desire to know Being impeded and indeed made impossible by the desire to know objects?

No doubt in his school, the Lyceum, Aristotle's original question of Being was pondered well. Yet in his lecture notes, the writings that have survived, he gives the impression that he has answered the question of Being when all he has done is give an account of the causes of beings. By so doing he prepared the stage for the dramatic entrance of Aquinas and Descartes: Aquinas, who after introducing Aristotelian categories to theology gave it all up in favor of direct, authentic knowledge, and Descartes, who solidified for subsequent Western thought the "clear and distinct" account of a subject "knowing" an object, a being knowing not Being but another being. The fateful error here is in thinking that by giving an inferential account of beings we now understand Being.

The so-called "two world" view of Plato needs to be understood as offering an analysis of two modes of knowing: an authentic, direct knowing of Being, and an inauthentic, indirect knowing of beings, the latter inauthentic not because of the ephemeral nature of sensory objects, as so many interpreters of Plato have maintained, but rather because of the desiring process, the ersatz self or being falsely believing it can know objects or beings, whereas in reality it can only identify with them, which far from being knowledge is simply ignorance.

What the Pythagorean school knew, and what Socrates and Plato knew, is that the ordinary mind or *ratio* is in service to desire, and that desire in its insidious sense is not simply the desire for this or that outcome or perceived good, but is rather the identification of our very being with an impulse to satisfy some need or privation. This identification or attachment is the process of desire at work in the human structure, and this process blinds us to our need for Being, here and now. And without a recognition of this process our very identity becomes invested in thought itself, or rather in the *content* of thought rather than in that higher Thought which is our awareness of what is.

Hence what comes to matter most, in the thrall of this process, is not Being itself but correct opinions or thoughts *about* Being or reality. This valuation of the content of thought is in direct opposition to the teaching of Socrates, as it is also opposed to the two principal schools of ancient Athens, the Academy of Plato and the Lyceum of Aristotle. For Socrates, as for Plato and Aristotle, this valuation was the greatest threat to the purpose of a school of thought, for it not only wrongly placed primary valuation upon speculative opinion but it also overlooked the dynamic of desire, and absent an understanding of that dynamic transformation of being was rendered impossible. And the liberation of thought itself depends upon an understanding of the process of desire.

The Development of Thought

Socrates, Plato, and Aristotle all knew that the development of real thought depended upon the development of being; thus, what was paramount in their respective schools was not the attainment of correct thought-content but the attainment of greater being, and this development was only possible in the school conditions created for that purpose. Each school had its own set of doctrines, but these ideas were not intended to function as unchallengeable dogmas but as catalysts for further thought in community and so for the transformation or development of the individual community members.

This notion of the development of thought being dependent upon the development of being is foreign to modern and postmodern thought, with rare exceptions. In the arena of academic philosophy, for example, a slight residue of communal effort still obtains in the limited classroom discussions and in the exchange of ideas among peers in academic journals. Yet any idea that all this activity is primarily for the purpose of developing being would seem odd at best, and would likely invite critical appraisal. What is emphasized is precisely what Socrates, Plato, and Aristotle wished to upend: the mistaken notion that what matters most is not being or thought itself but the content of thought, correct opinions about this or that dimension of reality.

The Tragic Poets

Another important element of ancient thought was the development of the presentation of tragedy on the stage, the plays of Sophocles, Aeschylus, and Euripides being among the most significant. Plato and Aristotle both had opinions about such productions, and both were intimately related to their belief that thought must not be in service to desire but in service to being.

Plato was opposed to the tragic poets, and to poetic activity generally, because he believed that such productions dramatized and in a sense glorified thought in service to desire; he felt that such dramatizations of the process of desire would inflame passions and do nothing to quiet the mind and still desire. Aristotle taught that tragic productions can have a cathartic effect, helping to purge negative and poisonous emotions from the audience and so promote a life of contemplation, thought in service to being.

We know that the tragic poets competed with one another and vied for prizes in producing the best plays. Were there also schools of thought associated with each major poet? We have no evidence that there were, but it would be in keeping with the ancient Greek tradition of communities of students forming around a major figure. Certainly the quality of thought in many of these productions indicates an effort to open questions of significance for human beings and think well about them, perhaps in community. Perhaps it would be instructive to consider one such question.

Sophocles' *Oedipus* is widely considered the most profound of ancient tragedies. It treats the human blindness so characteristic of intimate relationships, and its themes were advanced in another more modern sense by Freud. The question of human blindness to the identity of those closest to us resonates with the concern of ancient Greek thought about the blindness of ordinary thought or reason in service to desire. Oedipus unknowingly kills his father, weds his mother, and sires his siblings, and when he discovers the truth he blinds himself. Of course, this rupture of the communal fabric also issues in a curse upon the community itself, and this is once more in keeping with the impact upon both being and truth of a community's search for authentic thought. Hence it is possible to see in the presentation of this tragedy a product of communal thought regarding one of the more perplexing and difficult questions facing human beings, and how addressing this question can advance the more primordial question of human passion or desire. In so doing, it can also advance the attainment of authentic human thought and being.

The Hellenistic Schools

Alexander the Great was a pupil of Aristotle, and so a member of his school; Alexander's conquests mark the inception of the Hellenistic era, that period that lasted up until the advent of Roman dominance, the Greco-Roman era. The Hellenistic era was itself marked by a decline in formerly established ways of political governance, namely the temple-state and the polis, and an upsurge of esoteric schools devoted to the attainment of real knowledge and being.

Likely the best known school during these times was the Stoic; two of its more important adherents, Epictetus the slave and Marcus Aurelius the emperor, have left us writings indicating that during this time the Hellenistic schools took their place beside the Academy and the Lyceum, those schools begun by Plato and Aristotle and continuing into the Hellenistic era. Other well known schools include the Cynic and the Epicurean schools. Despite differences in doctrine, all of these schools excelled in training members in disciplines designed to develop both thought and being. Once again this highlights the fact that paramount in value in the conduct of these schools was transformation of being, not the attainment of correct opinions. As with the schools of Plato and Aristotle, doctrine was intended to be a catalyst for the development of authentic thought and being, not dogmas to be defended.

The Stoic school in particular was keen on studying and struggling with the process of desire. Higher mind, or *logos*, could be accessed only by questioning the fitness of the usual, ordinary mind, or *ratio*, to rule over the conflicting desires that bid for attention and satisfaction. Studying the process of desire or identification issued in a thought capable of transcending this process and forming needed connections with higher Thought. Stoics typically valued the quiet or still mind that is able to receive a higher influence, a higher Mind, that is the authentic Master or Ruler.

Plotinus

With the school of Plotinus we come upon the acme of Neoplatonic thought, the culmination of Platonic doctrine. Plotinus is the great nondual sage of Western thought, and through him Neoplatonism has had a decisive impact upon subsequent thought in the West. He is the most significant figure in the Imperial or Greco-Roman era following the Hellenistic period.

The primary interest in Plotinus' doctrine or thought was in keeping one's attention upon higher Mind; in order to attain this objective, one had to practice various forms of asceticism, a withdrawal of attention from the process of desire and the objects of desire. Through a process of development, one could then begin to recognize Being or Thought as one's authentic identity; without such a development on the intermediate level of being, one could not initiate this process of Self-realization. The impediment to such realization, here as elsewhere, was recognized to be desire or passion and those objects that promised satisfaction or happiness. One's real Identity is the nondual Being, and the aim of all real thought is to recognize or realize that Identity.

Thus the school of Plotinus, like the other schools we have examined, existed to further the development of the being of its members. It did not exist to indoctrinate its members with a specific set of ideas to be defended against all opposing notions, but to indicate the limitations of ideas in doing anything other than mutely pointing to reality in an invitation to taste and see for oneself. Such sacred ideas or doctrines were not intended to be verbal representations of reality. They were helps in stilling the ordinary mind and opening to higher Mind.

The Transition to Christianity

In the Imperial age the ancient schools of thought no longer discussed or pondered directly sacred ideas; instead, the discipline intended to help in the development of being and thought was the exegesis and interpretation of Neoplatonic ideas, the ideas of Plato, Plotinus, and other writers and their texts. This way of approaching serious thought liberated from desire in turn conditioned the subsequent thought of those pagans who converted to Christianity. Rather than directly addressing a particular idea such as the nature of reality, Imperial or Greco-Roman schools more indirectly addressed such an idea by consulting and interpreting a given text of Plato or Plotinus, for example. In this way subsequent Christian writers and thinkers were able to utilize ancient thought in a creative way, often more eisegesis than exegesis, yet once more the aim was the development of being and thought rather than the attainment of correct doctrine.

Eventually, however, Christian thought began to turn more toward a defense of key doctrines, and disputes within the Church over the correct content of doctrine began to replace a more fundamental search for being through ascetical practices, although the latter were continued in monastic settings and, to a lesser degree, in the earliest universities. Yet in the university settings we begin to detect a gradual shift of interest from inner development to the content of thought and doctrine, a shift from philosophy as a pursuit of wisdom to theology as a pursuit of "sound" doctrine.

Aristotle Misrepresented

Aristotle's school, like Plato's, valued developmental inquiry over established conclusions, doctrines, or results. Unfortunately, Christian Scholastics like Aquinas valued Aristotelian categories of thought more than inner development, except perhaps near the end of his career when he declared all his writings "as straw" when compared to his direct, immediate encounter with God.

Because Christian Scholastics like Thomas Aquinas only had access to Aristotle's lecture notes and apparently had little or no knowledge about the school conditions that likely obtained in Aristotle's Lyceum, Aristotle's attitude toward correct opinions was misrepresented as taking precedence over any concern for human development. As I have already observed, Aristotle's notes convey the impression that Being itself can be known by acquiring an uncertain, inferential knowledge of beings. Such a mistaken approach to knowledge eventually led to Aquinas' proofs for the existence of God.

By contrast, Augustine understood Being as a certain, direct knowledge of Awareness or Consciousness, and was not taken in by Aristotelian categories as Aquinas was. The Platonic idea that there is a direct and immediate knowledge of Being available to us was adopted by Augustine and introduced into the Christian worldview. Unfortunately, the Augustinian perspective was eclipsed by the supposedly Aristotelian approach among Christian Schoolmen.

Meister Eckhart and the Scholastics

Eckhart followed Aquinas in the university setting, and it was Eckhart who most faithfully forwarded the thought of Plotinus and Augustine about direct, immediate certainty of the knowledge of Being and about the necessity of development in the attainment of that end. Yet the more decisive influence belonged to Scholastics like Aquinas, those Schoolmen who continued the heritage of Aristotelian categories combined with the notion of the revelation of the Logos into the modern university setting.

What, then, if anything, happened to the ascetic practice of spiritual disciplines intended to foster inner development and eventual Self-realization? Such practices were more and more confined to monastic enclaves. Outside the walls of the monastery, Western thought followed more closely the Scholastic interest in philosophy as the handmaid of theology, an interest in thought more as received content or doctrine than in thought as fostering a development of being. And with this growing medieval development we enter into the university setting of modern times, characterized by a loss of interest in the ultimate concern of authentic thought.

The Ancient Quest For Being

The ancient quest for Being within the different schools of thought in the West was also a quest for certainty, certainty both in knowledge and in being, for the two are one.

Both the doctrines adopted by a given school of thought and the dialogues or discussions sparked by those sacred ideas functioned as spiritual exercises or disciplines intended to foster a development of being, a development of certainty. Thus from the inception of Western thought the quest for certainty in being or knowledge required a development in being, itself needed to attain certainty. Yet the certainty attained was not certain knowledge in the sense of verbal descriptions or representations of reality; instead, it was a certainty attained by becoming, or being, reality itself.

Being and certainty, then, was from the start inextricably tied to becoming or development. And neither being nor becoming was dependent upon the attainment of correct doctrines about reality. Verbal accounts or doctrines about reality served only to initiate a process of development on the intermediate level of being, a development that would eventually issue in certain knowledge – not *about* reality, but in *being* reality.

One's real Identity, as Plotinus would maintain, is always already here and now; the difficulty is that without a further development of being on an intermediate level between one's socially conditioned feeling of self and the authentic Self-feeling, one's *feeling* of identity remains bound by and bound to ordinary feelings, thoughts, and sensations. School conditions and disciplines are needed to challenge this mistaken feeling and also to begin the process of self-initiation into an altogether different and higher feeling of self. For that initiation school conditions are established to develop a new feeling of self, of identity, one that vibrates in harmony with the authentic Identity and that can form a connection to it.

The Role Of Ordinary Thought

Just as members of these ancient schools began with an ordinary feeling of self or identity, so they also began their development with ordinary thought or reason. What they had trouble seeing was how their usual thought was enslaved by their usual feeling of self and how this feeling of 'I' was at the root of the process of desire.

Ancient schools of thought, beginning with these facts, initiated their members into a study of this mistaken state of affairs. The Western approach began with this ordinary feeling of 'I' and the ordinary thought orbiting it, challenging both with doctrines that fostered deep questioning both of thought and of identity. In Plato's myth of the cave, for example, members of the Academy were led to question the quality of their experience, and to doubt as well the ability of their usual thought to reason well about such experience, to come to correct conclusions about reality itself. Hellenistic and Greco-Roman schools would build upon this myth, engaging thought in an interrogation of thought itself. And in so doing their unquestioned feeling of self, their identity, would also be interrogated.

During this process of development, one's realization of a lack of understanding, of knowing, signaled the birth of understanding, of knowing, of higher being. School aspirants began to feel the poverty of their usual thought, their mistaken identity, the privation of their being. What was needed, they began to feel, was a finer thought, an authentic identity, a development of being. In recognizing their privation, they recognized their need, and began to value what would meet that need: Being itself.

Such recognition challenged once and for all the hegemony of desire. Ordinary thought, in service to contradictory desires, reinforced the ersatz feeling of 'I' and did nothing to emancipate itself. Yet ancient schools used this thought, guided by school elders and school disciplines, to come to an understanding of its own poverty, its own enslavement. For this to occur, school conditions had to prevail.

School Conditions

The absolutely essential requirement for the liberation of thought is the establishment and maintenance of school conditions, the way of life, of communal life, established by school masters, teachers, or elders. By oneself nothing can be attained, no real development of being, no development of a feeling for a finer thought.

This fact obtains because ordinary thought falsely claims hegemony over the human structure. No other candidate for rulership presents itself. One needs special help to begin to understand the fundamental existential predicament. Because the usual feeling of 'I' is persuaded by thought's claim, the latter is never challenged by the former, nor the former by the latter. An outside force is needed to challenge both, and that force begins to be felt within the protected boundaries of an authentic school of inner work.

As this indispensable requirement for development began to weaken in the West, the interest in reason or thought itself began to capitulate to the desire to know the truth, to know reality, not from a developed state of being so much as from a putatively elevated position of knowing. A primordial interest in Being or ontology gradually gave way to an interest in ways of knowing, in epistemology. The quest for certainty shifted from the developing being to correct beliefs or opinions about how to be certain, how to know.

Resignation

Because of this shift, Western thought moved inexorably toward a resignation about the limitations of thought or reason. Having lost the ontological key to authentic thought, knowledge, and certainty, Western thinkers, in investigating ways of knowing, began to recognize ever more deeply the poverty of ordinary thought.

Eventually, some of the best thinkers of modern times were led reluctantly to the conclusion seen long ago in ancient times: that our usual thought is slave to our passions, our desires. Unfortunately, the *process* of desire, of identification, continued to work unrecognized, furthering the mistrust in reason or thought to attain knowledge or certainty at all. We will explore this development further in the next chapter.

CHAPTER THREE

MODERN WESTERN THOUGHT

Cartesian Doubt

With Rene Descartes we enter the birth of modern philosophizing, characterized by a turn from ontology to epistemology, from a primary interest in Being to a primary interest in knowing. That these two, knowing and Being, are one, was not apparent to thinkers from Descartes on.

Descartes' lasting legacy was his pursuit of certainty, actually a pursuit of Being, but thought by him to be a quest for certain knowledge, obtainable by ordinary reason, disconnected from the other sources of knowing in our being. He was determined to find certain *contents* of thought, truths that could be without question articulated with certainty. What he discovered was the truth of thinking itself, leading to the undoubted truth of his own being: I think, therefore I am.

One can see in this articulation a degeneration of thought: thought is separated from Being, and is thought to demonstrate Being. Thought is no longer recognized as Being itself; hence, ordinary thought, or reason, is posited as Thought or Awareness, Consciousness itself. This advent of rationalism elevates ordinary thought into a position properly reserved for Seeing, a Thought that is Consciousness in the sense of higher Attention, a property not of the social self but of the real Self. Ordinary thought is placed on a pedestal from which it will be toppled in due course.

In this epistemological turn from Being to ordinary knowing, one observes how an absence of school conditions invites a faulty quest for certainty. Absent sacred ideas or doctrines shared within the protected boundaries of an organized school of inner work, an enslaved faculty of the mind is elevated to a position rightfully due to authentic Thought only.

Hume's Critique of Self and Causality

The toppling of ordinary thought, and the resignation toward what such thought can and cannot attain, begins in earnest with the thought of David Hume. He agrees with the other empiricists that our knowledge comes through the observation of our senses, but he wonders how rationalists like Descartes as well as his fellow empiricists like Berkeley are able to observe an 'I'. Where is this 'I' or self that Descartes believes is demonstrated by thought?

Hume concludes that such a self cannot be observed, and hence ordinary thought cannot with integrity posit it. All that can be observed, he writes, is a bundle of sensations called thoughts, emotions, and somatic "raw feels" like itches or pains. Although this conclusion appears to be in agreement with certain schools of Eastern thought, like Buddhism, it is actually in disagreement with the vast majority of Eastern schools, and also reveals the need for an organized inner work; had Hume had access to such a school, his observations would have been able to be deeper and more complete.

Hume then goes on to critique the notion of causality, so necessary to what was in his day the developing enterprise of natural science. Scientific thought claims to observe one thing causing another, but Hume maintains that no such observation can be conducted; rather, what can be observed is one thing following another, and in that observation there can be no secure promise that the next time the thing that followed another this time will again follow. And, like the self, because the supposed cause cannot be observed it cannot with integrity be posited, throwing into doubt the entire enterprise of scientific thought.

Yet Hume was a gentle soul, and did not wish to distress. Nor did he wish to press his skeptical conclusions. Instead, he counseled one and all to relax and enjoy life to the degree possible, knowing that our thought life was properly subsumed within our wishes and desires. The examples of our mistaken belief in a self and in causality furnished relatively unimportant instances of how our passions or desires dominate our thought life, for it is out of our wish for a self and for there to be a causal explanation for the world's natural processes that lead us to conclusions unsupported by a more careful examination. Ordinary thought, or reason, he wrote, is slave to our passions, and it is our passions that provide the fundamental motivation to act and fulfill our desires. For Hume, that is thought's useful and proper place. The pursuit of critique, of more careful thought, was itself, for Hume, a pleasant pastime; he did not expect others to share this interest.

Hume's denial of all knowledge is mitigated by his conviction that our lives are not based upon our intellectual conclusions, or reasons for believing this or accepting that, but rather upon our desires. The quest for certainty in knowledge begun by the rationalist Descartes could be said to end with the empiricist Hume, who maintained we can never be sure of anything, not the existence of God, the external world, causality or reliable connections among objects or beings, or indeed ourselves as selves. For Hume, the ends of our behavior are set by our desires; reason comes in to rationalize and secure those ends.

Once again, the trajectory of Western thought highlights the necessity of beginning, not with reason, but with desire, recognizing that no certainty is possible without first addressing the truth or falsity of the desiring process. Hume never questioned this process, just accepted it as a fact of human nature, and resigned himself to the apparent truth that reason can only be in service to desire. Thus for Hume so-called "theories of everything" are out of the question, for if we cannot be certain of or know anything we can never have an answer to everything.

Kant's Critiques of Reason

Immanuel Kant was not so sanguine about Hume's skeptical conclusions; for Kant Newtonian science was our only source of certain knowledge, and for this to be thrown into doubt was intolerable. For Kant Newtonian science was the proper response to the wonder evoked by the "starry sky without." Kant yearned for Cartesian certainty but could not ignore Hume's conclusions.

So how to account for the certainty felt in the Newtonian account of the universe? If our certainty is dependent upon a direct observation of causal events "out there," then our entire feeling of security in such a scientific account is mistaken and we are as adrift upon a sea of uncertainty as our ancient hunting and gathering ancestors were. Kant's solution to this difficulty played a major role in the West's ongoing resignation to what thought could and could not attain.

Kant maintained that our thought led to Hume's conclusions because we have misunderstood the role of thought itself; we have been picturing our minds as a passive mirror receiving images from the outer world, and the truth or falsity, the certainty or uncertainty, of our knowledge depends upon the accuracy of that reception, how truly representative the images are to what caused them. The reason causality cannot be observed is because it is not a property of reality "out there": it is a property of our minds. We impose the notion of causality necessarily; it is the only way possible for us to perceive and come to know the phenomenal world. But what the world is in itself, what is really the case apart from our minds, we can never know.

So ends Kant's first critique of reason or thought. We do indeed have certainty, but not about reality: we have certainty about how reality appears to us. We must, then, be resigned to this reduced role of thought to know the real, precisely in order to rescue certainty and so the legitimacy of our scientific enterprise. With this critique Kant brought to an abrupt halt most metaphysical treatises on the nature of reality.

Kant's second critique treats the second cause of wonder: the moral law within. Just as we have a feeling of certainty about natural law, so we have a feeling of certainty about our unconditional freedom to will the good. With this critique Kant attempts to rescue humanity from the clutches of scientific determinism, for according to the latter we are determined in all our choices and actions. Yet this cannot be, wrote Kant, because once again the question of certainty is at stake, as well as our freedom of will.

Recall that Hume resigned himself to the fact that our thought is in service to our passions. A careful examination of the doctrine of scientific determinism, widely accepted at that time, would also hold that our wishes, motivations, desires, are also determined, caused by impulses and forces beyond our control. Where, in this "certain" scientific thought, is there room for freedom of will and action? In agreement with ancient Western thought, Kant argued that our free will, our wish to serve higher Thought, revealed a part of our nature untouched by the laws of science. He in effect agreed with Plato regarding the twofold nature of the human being.

Kant maintained that to actualize this wish for the good or higher one must discount personal or egoic desire. In place of obeying the lower nature and its laws one obeys the higher and its laws. Not occupying a place of self-study and discipline in a spiritual school, Kant relies on different "maxims" to remind himself and others about the freedom to will the good rather than succumb to the usual impulses and desires. The most familiar is the categorical imperative, which to paraphrase is to act as if universally legislating for all.

The third critique attempts to provide a unifying or reconciling force in the experience of beauty. For Kant, contemplation of beauty is the closest one can come to reconciling the lower with the higher, for it is itself the incarnation in form of the good, the higher. And with this experience we come full circle back to where we started: the experience of wonder, wonder at the starry sky above and the moral law within.

Kant's Legacy to Western Thought

Kant's decisive legacy to Western thought, despite his attempts to rescue us from science and its causal clutches, is a pervasive resignation about the ability of reason or ordinary thought to attain knowledge of the real, of Being. For despite all the chatter about Being contained in the works of subsequent thinkers like Heidegger and Sartre, the reach of reason or thought can never surpass the phenomenal realm; we can only know Being as it appears to us, not as it might be in itself. Heidegger once observed that "I am too much of a Kantian" to think otherwise. Thus his being "on the way to Being" cannot promise a direct knowledge of Being itself.

Under the spell of this legacy, the possibility of any sort of thought to receive a direct and so veridical impression of the Real, of Being, never surfaces in the post-critical, post-Kantian world of Western thought. Often thought is snubbed in favor of another human faculty, usually feeling. The thought of most modern and postmodern artists, the thought expressed in painting, sculpture, and literature, usually favors this romantic turn to the passions or desires. What is true of one sort of thought, ordinary thought, is assumed true of all possible thought.

What has been lost is the teaching of ancient Western schools that while thought in service to desire is severely limited and enslaved, it is possible, given the right conditions, to open to and receive a higher Thought or Attention, a higher energy that can unify and transform. Under this Thought or Awareness the lower functions of ordinary thought, feeling, and somatic sensation and instinctual impulses can be harmonized and in turn serve higher purposes than those served by the process of desire.

Thus the decisive moment in Western thought came when Kant declared that we possess no somatic instruments for knowing the real, what he called the noumenon, only for knowing phenomena, appearances.

Schopenhauer

Schopenhauer presents an interesting post-critical – that is, post-Kantian – thinker, for he is the first major thinker or philosopher in the West who had access to some of the wisdom literature of the East, the Upanishads and Buddhist texts.

Schopenhauer believed that he had reached similar conclusions independently of the Eastern literature he later encountered, but his pessimism ran counter to the spirit of Eastern wisdom as reflected in the few texts then available in the West. He was by and large a Kantian, yet levied some appropriate critiques at Kant's thought, the most devastating of which was asking what gave Kant the audacity to posit a "thing-in-itself" as the cause of phenomena? Causality was supposed to be a category imposed by our limited minds, one of the necessary shapers of our experience. Using this category to explain anything outside of phenomenal experience is, then, to use a phenomenal feature to trespass onto noumenal territory.

His own attempt to combine Kant's notion of a transcendent will with Eastern teaching about the great Self or Reality led Schopenhauer to posit a "Will" that was more like a mindless Force than anything we would recognize as a will. It was this Force or Will that he believed was the noumenon or Reality behind our phenomenal experience, and, as such, could never be known or understood. This conclusion of his is indeed Kantian but hardly Eastern. By contrast, Eastern teachings, as we will see in a later chapter, maintain that the Real can be both known and understood, and is indeed Thought itself. But not known in a scientific, scholarly, or subject-object sense, for that is only uncertain opinion, to use Plato's language. Rather, it is knowing Being by *being* Being, recognizing Being *as* Being.

Schopenhauer did agree with Eastern thought in writing that "so long as we are given up to the throng of desires . . . we never obtain lasting happiness or peace." Thus he believed that desire must be repudiated; however, not having the good fortune to belong to a school of inner work intended to find liberation from desire, he wrote that we can only find "momentary release" from the meaninglessness of existence through the contemplation of art. Weak tea indeed compared to the strong soma-drink of spiritual schools.

Goethe

Western, and in particular German, thought has been decisively influenced by the greatest German poet and man of letters, Goethe, for it was he who impressed upon an entire culture the importance and indeed the necessity of development.

Crucial as this influence is, Goethe's writings dismiss the ancient Western idea of the two natures of men and women as well as their possible reconciliation. This dismissal is most unfortunate, for the development most needed in the human structure is one that reconciles the lower with the higher, the terrestrial and the celestial natures of man.

Goethe also questioned the ancient idea that men and women have an essence, a more essential being that is veiled by the socially conditioned sense of self. His thought was radical in that he questioned the belief that man has a self at all. Instead, he believed that the self was a shorthand way of referring to an individual's deeds and creations, and that it was the latter especially that revealed one's development, both as a human being and as a creator, an artist.

Whereas his contemporary Kant lauded Newtonian science as our only certain access to knowledge, Goethe became the fountainhead for a different conception of science, a poetic science that did not rely on mathematics. This idea has borne much fruit, and in the thought of Nietzsche it was developed into a profound psychology of masks while in Freud it came to full fruition as the poetic science of psychoanalysis. Philosophers Paul Ricoeur and Walter Kaufmann both considered the Freudian achievement as a practical development of Goethe's initial vision of a nonmathematical science.

Although Goethe was interested in advancing his notion of a poetic science, in direct opposition to Kant he was dismissive of the idea of a quest for certainty in knowledge. Abandoning the ancient search for certainty, Goethe praised a developmental approach of advancing and testing hypotheses, an idea that resonates better with post-Newtonian science than Kant's belief that Newtonian science was certain, needing no further testing.

Reconciling Kant and Goethe

Several subsequent thinkers attempted to reconcile the thought of Kant and Goethe, primarily because they sensed an incompleteness in both. In Kant, they felt insufficient interest in development; in Goethe, insufficient interest in certainty. Among these thinkers are names like Hegel, Kierkegaard, Husserl, and Heidegger.

Attempts at reconciling Kant and Goethe are doomed to fail, however, because both men misunderstood how the ancient Western thinkers reconciled being and becoming, certainty and development. Certainty and development were inextricably fused in an overall existential way of life conducted in the ancient schools of thought. Certainty was attained through development of being, while further development was guided by certainty; development, that is, depends upon infusions of being, while receptivity to being depends upon development. There is thus a reciprocal and necessary relationship between being and becoming, certainty and development. The notion that being and becoming are in opposition or conflict is an idea that takes hold only when these school conditions are not understood as the absolutely essential safeguards of a process of discovery and development.

Hegel is one philosopher who attempted a reconciliation of Kant and Goethe. For Hegel individual development is not possible unless such a one becomes an integral part of an "organic society." He located certainty or Being in an overarching process of development: reality is the Spirit in manifestation or development, destined to lead to individual and societal harmony. In this conception Being itself is temporalized; Being is subject to becoming. A colossal attempt to reconcile Kant and Goethe, to be sure, but one which fails to comprehend how being and becoming are two names for one reality, and how they are necessarily and reciprocally related. Above all, Hegel placed an altogether undeserved trust in the conceptual mind and in the ability of concepts to disclose or, to use Heidegger's term, "reveal" truth.

Schopenhauer is another thinker who tried to reconcile the legacies of Kant and Goethe, and no less a philosopher than Ludwig Wittgenstein believed that Schopenhauer's conclusions about reality or the way the world is was correct and marked a definite end to Western metaphysics. All that remained, for Wittgenstein, was to clear up a few traditional pseudo-problems of Western philosophy and after that to make Western thought more edifying.

Postmodern Thought

Richard Rorty's classic *Philosophy and the Mirror of Nature* characterizes truly postmodern thought as being "edifying" rather than "systematic," and lists such edifying thinkers as Wittgenstein, Heidegger, and John Dewey as harbingers of a kind of Western thought liberated from the oppressive demand of attaining truth.

What displaces a concern for truth, and especially a quest for certainty, is a concern for the advancement of civil conversation, where interlocutors can engage in spirited exchange without the overhead of reaching anything resembling certainty. This approach in itself, Rorty maintains, produces better listeners.

Obviously not all postmodern thinkers in the West have abandoned truth as a matter of ultimate concern in favor of engaged, and engaging, conversation. But Rorty's viewless view is emblematic of the postmodern turn from absolute truth to relative perspectives. It is a form of pragmatism that disowns the popular pragmatic criterion of truth, and indeed snubs any theory of truth.

Ironically, some pragmatists have captured essential truths that were practiced in ancient schools; no better example of this irony is Dewey's *A Theory of Valuation*, which maintains that authentic valuation is grounded upon a felt recognition of privation or need, precisely the teaching found in ancient Western schools of thought. And the American pragmatist C.S. Pierce believed that we are moved to know through the perception of some need or lack.

With this insight Western pragmatists are very close to Eastern and some currents of Western esoteric thought: a need, lack, or privation is discovered or felt which motivates us to look for whatever knowledge or help will fill that need, and we are willing to learn from those who have already made that discovery. Knowledge is an activity, said Pierce, and we obtain knowledge by being participants, not spectators.

In this regard knowledge is useful in meeting need, only this "pragmatic principle" is easily coopted by desire, the very human process that itself needs to be examined and known before need can be intelligently met. Here again, absent knowledge of how the mind works, thought intended to meet need is instead coopted by desire, and is thus deflected from its intended outcome of useful knowledge, knowledge that actually meets need.

The Puzzle of Greek Tragedy

Greek and Elizabethan tragedies are puzzling: they present on stage extreme suffering, yet audiences return again and again to view them with satisfaction. How to account for this apparent anomaly?

Two modern thinkers, Nietzsche and Schopenhauer, have offered diametrically opposed accounts of this anomaly, both having considerable bearing on our examination of Western thought. Schopenhauer maintained that audiences were obliged to face the absurdity and meaninglessness of life, and in so doing were granted a brief respite from it, in effect withdrawing their usual affection for life and experiencing a temporary taste of detachment.

Schopenhauer was one of Nietzsche's "educators," but his first book, *The Birth of Tragedy*, heralded his emancipation from the former's world-weary resignation. In that book Nietzsche argued that in Greek tragedy the absurdity and horror of existence was transfigured by art, and life itself justified as an aesthetic phenomenon. He also maintained that tragedy died from Socratic rationalism, and in his work on Nietzsche Heidegger advanced this thesis by claiming that the elevation of reason by philosophers from Plato to Nietzsche was a "fateful error" that could only be remedied by a contemplation of Greek thought before the advent of Socrates. That Socrates was himself opposed to that sort of ersatz rationalism neither Nietzsche nor Heidegger understood.

Authentic, liberated reason requires the participation and harmonization of the entire structure of a given human being, and this harmonization and participation is itself dependent upon a conscious divestment of trust in an ersatz rationalism, the reason of the disconnected intellect, interested primarily not in Thought or Being but in the content of Thought, in ordinary thought, in thoughts. And it is this interest, according to Nietzsche and Heidegger, that led to the death of tragedy, for what this sort of rationalism teaches is that with reason one can avoid tragedy.

Disconnected Thought

Thus only one form of thought or reason is incompatible with seeing life as beautiful, as an aesthetic phenomenon, despite its horror and suffering: the thought of the disconnected, unsubmitted mind. And although Plato saw himself as a rival of the tragic poets, and of poets in general, it was not because he believed poets were either rational or irrational; rather, it was because he believed an individual's time and energy should be devoted to the discovery and development of Being, and that spiritual disciplines intended to foster that aim were to be practiced within the protected boundaries of a school of inner work; viewing dramatizations of the process of desire was simply not recommended. It may be, of course, that Plato insufficiently appreciated the humanizing effect of such dramatizations, but the authentic reason cultivated by a school like the Academy had nothing to do with a supposed inability to consider life beautiful.

Schopenhauer exemplifies how disconnected thought can issue in such an inability. He came to negative conclusions about the absurdity of life, and after reading Eastern spiritual texts felt validated about those conclusions. Having access to no organized spiritual school, he was unable to understand how such thought itself needs liberation, and how without a development of authentic feeling one can never recognize beauty, truth, and goodness even in the teeth of absurdity. As I mentioned before, Schopenhauer believed in the ability of beauty, of art, to offer a brief respite from absurdity, but this was only a feeling for the beautiful or sublime, not a feeling that reveals truth or goodness. The so-called "Will" or Reality proclaimed by Schopenhauer is a blind Force with no possible connection to the human predicament. The case of Schopenhauer illustrates how essential school conditions are to an authentic understanding of the real and so also the liberation of thought.

The Socratic Ethos

The Socratic ethos and the ethos of the tragic Greek poets are identical. Both emerge from a pervasive disillusionment about a life ruled by the process of desire. In one case, that of Socrates, disillusionment issues in a persistent questioning of such a life; in the other, that of the tragic poets, disillusionment issues in a transfiguration of such a life on stage. Both are creative responses to the apparent absurdity of existence.

Both also invite participants to a fuller involvement in and engagement with life. In the case of the tragic poets the participants are primarily the actors playing their given roles, but there is also a demand for fuller participation levied upon the audience. And as I surmised in the previous chapter, there was likely a spiritual school with devoted followers gathered around tragic poets like Sophocles.

What is decidedly *not* characteristic of either schools like Plato's Academy or the creations of the tragic poets is the medieval, modern, and postmodern exercise of a disconnected reason. Without a teaching about the help needed from above, from the real, thought separated from other organs of knowing in the human structure presents itself as the master, particularly in those cultures where the isolated intellect has been cultivated to the neglect of feeling, instinct, and somatic sensation.

What has happened is that modern and postmodern maladies have been projected back onto ancient cultures. Thus thinkers like Nietzsche and Heidegger dupe themselves and others into believing that the ancient Western thinkers elevated an ersatz reason into the ruling faculty of the human frame, when in fact this elevation did not obtain until the understanding of the essential role of school conditions upon the authentic discovery and development of objective reason was lost.

Existentialism

One modern, Western tradition of thought that makes all others appear dry and academic is known as existentialism. Existentialism maintains that serious thought needs to begin with extreme situations, with what philosopher Walter Kaufmann called life at the limits, the same sort of existential realities that attract the attention not only of certain types of philosophers, writers, and artists but also tragic poets and religious or spiritual figures. Compared to existentialism, other traditions of Western thought like logical positivism, analytical philosophy, phenomenology, structuralism and post-structuralism, seem arid and lifeless.

What is it about existentialism that attracts so many divergent thinkers in so many different disciplines and fields? Why does it hold such appeal to young people who are struggling with the very questions that deeply touch their lives and often leave them despairing of hope for answers? The answer to these questions resides in the state of being to which we are called in the teeth of extremity: facing extreme situations like death and destitution, feeling often overwhelming emotions like dread and despair, a demand to collect ourselves into a more gathered state of attention becomes a necessary part of such experiences, and in such a state we find ourselves more awake with far more vivid feelings of being alive. Despite the fact that we would much rather avoid extreme situations and feelings, the additional fact remains that relative to more usual states of being or awareness this more collected state is the very paradigm of what it can mean to be intensely alive.

It is this state of intensity that so attracts us. And perhaps we come to feel that most of our lives are spent in states that by comparison seem automatic, dull, and perfunctory. We enjoy reading tales about those in extremity, we enjoy going to plays and movies depicting extreme situations, we may deliberately put ourselves in situations that although present no real danger to us still get our adrenalin going, all to feel more alive and provide some respite from lackluster routine.

Intensity and Serenity

One very interesting existentialist poet, Rainer Maria Rilke, composed several poems exploring the possible reconciliation of two human experiences that at first appear opposed: intensity and serenity. Yet this opposition is an appearance only, is only conceptual.

The compatibility of intensity and serenity found in Eastern thought will have to wait to be examined in a later chapter. For now, we confine ourselves to Western thought, where examples of this compatibility abound. Perhaps the best example is to be found in Plato's *Apology*, where the serene Socrates faces his death with composure and aplomb, yet with an unforgettable intensity of feeling and purpose. He was able to combine intensity and serenity not because he was exceptional by nature but because of his own discovery and development, discovery of help above and development of being below.

The intensity and serenity of a Socrates inspired not only Plato and his Academy but also all subsequent schools of thought in the West. Sophocles and the other tragic poets dramatized the intensity of being evoked by extremity, but such intense being in the face of extremity did not include serenity; rather, what was depicted on stage was emotional intensity, a state of being that, although strongly collected and powerful, was still ruled by desire, by passion. The tragic protagonist was still in service to a social sense of self, the ordinary identity, and the extreme events to which the protagonist was exposed also exposed this fragile self-sense, touching it to the core. Such an identity is prey to despair, guilt, and dread, what Kierkegaard called the sickness unto death.

While such intensity is far preferable to the soporific state of being that characterizes ordinary life, it is no safeguard against the potentially destructive emotions that can sweep away a socially conditioned sense of identity into madness or even death. What is wanted is a practical way to come to a state of intense aliveness without being dependent upon extreme situations or emotions. And it is this intense aliveness, compatible with an abiding serenity, that was cultivated in the spiritual schools of discovery and development.

Existential Understanding

The intensity of being and feeling that is evoked by extremity is a product of a gathered state of attention with the concomitant harmonization of thought, feeling, and somatic sensation-movement. And the reason people continue to seek such intensity either vicariously or by courting semblances of extremity is because they have been conditioned to anticipate such vividness and also because they know no other way to feel intensely alive.

Spiritual schools, ancient, medieval, modern, and contemporary, possess the existential understanding that not only makes the pursuit of intensity unnecessary but that also exposes it as an importantly paradigmatic example of how thought can be blinded by desire, in this case the desire for a fuller, more vivid experience of life. And it is just here where a study of the process of desire can fruitfully begin.

An aspirant entering a spiritual school must begin with the understanding available, most often a product of social conditioning. Such an individual may wish to escape suffering, may be disillusioned with life, or may have one or more other motivations leading to entering school conditions. For the sake of developing the above example, let's say an individual enters a school in order to live a more intense, fulfilling life. Perhaps the aspirant has sufficient experience in extreme situations to know that either viewing them dramatized or actually undergoing them has evoked an intense state of being or presence that differs substantially from one's usual, more fragmented states, and perhaps one even senses that there is another, though analogous, possibility that a greater understanding could disclose.

The Study of Desire

The aspirant, then, enters a disciplined way of life with a desire for a certain result or outcome. That individual is then gradually reoriented from aiming at the outcome to the desire itself, from a future hope to a present reality. Soon enough discrimination begins to arise: a distinction is developed between the thought or thoughts that orbit one's particular desire for a result or outcome, thoughts in service to that desire, and the Thought or Attention that observes that desire and those thoughts, that considers them, that studies them, not in order to get anywhere or to attain some result, but simply to watch, to be aware – in fact *to be* rather than to be this or that.

So Being itself shows itself as the value that is needed: not the ersatz value of being this or that, but just *being*. And at the same time one becomes aware of a development: the *development* of being, of the capacity to be aware, or rather of the capacity to recognize awareness, to feel awareness or attention as one's ownmost identity. The aspirant, entering with the usual mistaken sense of self and ruled by desires for results, begins to understand how this mistaken self-sense and those desires occlude the obvious reality of Being, the only certainty and the only development, the only being and the only becoming, that can yield the only attainable intensity and serenity possible for a human being.

Given time, the school aspirant understands that in discovering and developing Being, one's intermediate level of being, one finds and invites the serenity needed to withstand even the intensity of extreme situations. For the development of being necessarily includes the connections established among the usually fragmented centers of intelligence in the human frame – the centers of mind, feeling, and body – and with their connection their harmonization. Serenity is required because a connection between mind and body demands a quieting of the usually noisy head brain, a quieting of ordinary, desire-driven thought. And the discovery of Being and the development of being necessarily includes the discovery of authentic Thought and the development or cultivation of a more liberated thought, an attention that can receive a higher Attention or Awareness.

Scientific Thought

Western thinkers have been decisively influenced by the birth and development of science, and the protocols of science have often become the model of what is considered rigorous thought. We have already seen how the problems that occupied thinkers like Hume and Kant were those that were occasioned by reflecting upon the enterprise of science and the reasoning needed to attain scientific progress. Nineteenth-century thinkers believed that science was a source of certain, incorrigible knowledge, thus perpetuating Kant's mistaken view. But with the revolutionary theories of relativity and quantum mechanics, this prevailing view lost favor.

In the 20th century especially, serious thinkers found themselves reflecting upon the protocols of science in an attempt to account for its apparent domination of Western thought and culture. Although difficult to single out a representative figure in this complex setting, perhaps philosopher of science Karl Popper would serve to illustrate how the West thought the enterprise of science was conducted.

Popper conceived of the conduct and progress of science as a matter of conjectures and refutations. Scientific experiments are conducted, observations made, and, in the absence of an already accepted hypothesis or theory, a conjecture is offered which, if fruitful, is readily available either for confirmation or refutation. Others perform similar experiments in order to test the hypothesis, and, with sufficient confirmations and no decisive refutations, the conjecture becomes tentatively accepted as a temporary way to account for the observations that first led to the conjecture. Because of the problem of induction — because no such conjecture can be definitively verified — no one who understands scientific thought believes that a given conjecture is decidedly established as true. That belief was the mistake Kant made regarding Newtonian science.

What is most important to understand about scientific thought is that for science reality is theoretical only, and the final arbiter of theoretical "truth" is not experience but the experiment. For that reason a great deal of Western thought in the 20th and 21st centuries, modeled upon scientific and mathematical reasoning, seems remote from life, forming a very different tradition than existential thought, and appealing to a very different sort of person than one interested in existentialism. Of course there are exceptions, such as Wittgenstein, who was interested in both. But the vast majority of thinkers who are engaged in reflection about how logic and language shape our experience of life are very dissimilar to those thinkers who begin their thinking from a consideration of extreme situations.

Scientific reasoning, and the problems of logic and language that interest those who have been influenced by a tradition of thought in turn shaped by science and mathematics, can of course be a particularly fascinating way of using a clever mind without ever questioning one's being or identity. Consequently there is another tradition of thought in the West that critiques the former interest as overlooking the more important human questions.

Continental Thought

Most Anglo-American philosophy follows in the tradition of an interest in logic and language, while the tradition that follows a more existential interest is by and large confined to the continent of Europe. We can consider two representative figures of this latter interest to illustrate their concerns and their critiques.

Kierkegaard critiques Hegel's system of thought as being too abstract, remote from life, and this feature of Hegel's thought is due to his attempt to reconcile Goethe and Kant. Hegel took Goethe's emphasis upon development and gave it a Kantian spin, both in writing style and in conception, in effect trying to marry development and certainty.

It was precisely this feature of Hegel's philosophy that Kierkegaard critiqued, maintaining that both development and certainty in abstract thought did justice neither to development nor to certainty. Kierkegaard wrote that certainty in particular could never be attained in abstract thinking, and that faith alone, characterized as a "leap," could supply certainty. Absolute truth can only be subjective, Kierkegaard said emphatically, and this truth can only be approached through the most intense self-examination and self-study.

Kierkegaard also wrote about extreme states of being, like despair and dread, and it was from him that Heidegger derived his own critique of abstract thinking in the latter's *Being and Time*, without acknowledging his debt to Kierkegaard. Heidegger maintained that an interest in extremity, an interest in one's being toward death, for example, was a way to approach Being itself. In this he was in agreement with other more existential thinkers like Sartre, who wrote his own *Being and Nothingness* under the influence of Heidegger's work.

What is most interesting about Sartre's thought is his questioning of his own abstractions, a continuation of the legacy of Kant. In his essays, novels, and plays Sartre wishes to find a way to convey the existential dimension of life without reliance upon "words, words, words." Such questioning highlights the paradox of saying, as Heidegger did, that abstract thinking about Being can lead to the meaning of Being. Heidegger's later thought abandons this unhelpful idea in favor of a hermeneutical approach to texts as another possible way to "reveal" Being itself. Yet no other existential thinker has so precisely put the futility of abstract thinking as Kierkegaard: that it reveals neither Being nor Truth.

Western Esoteric Thought

With the rise and development of state-sanctioned Christianity spiritual schools like that of Plotinus and other Neoplatonic thinkers had to run for cover.

Christianity became more and more dogmatic and intolerant of divergent thought, so any surviving schools of necessity had to operate in secret, and in so doing became esoteric, hidden from the Christian majority.

During the advent of the Renaissance an abiding interest in combining different schools of thought like Alexandrian Hermeticism, Kabbalah, and Paracelsian *Naturphilosophie* obtained among thinkers like Ficino and Mirandola. Perhaps the most important idea taken from ancient Western thought was that of the microcosm, the notion of a correspondence between higher and lower, and more specifically the idea that a human being is a *potential* microcosm, a mirror of the entire cosmos.

This idea naturally comported well with the ancient emphasis upon a development of being: in order to actualize this potential, development is required. And for this development a school is needed, a community wherein conditions can be established and sustained, conditions essential to this development, this actualization.

Correspondences were also found among apparently differing parts or levels of the cosmos: correspondences between the transmutation of metals and the transmutation of the human being, for example. In this regard the tradition of alchemy forms one of the more interesting examples of esoteric Western thought. In alchemy, as in other esoteric traditions, symbols of transmutation were used at once to communicate to those who had been initiated into the tradition and to hide the real meaning from those who had not been so initiated.

Freud's erstwhile follower C. G. Jung made an extensive study of alchemy, recognized the symbolic nature of its writings, but misread the literal truth to which the symbols pointed. He assumed the alchemists were simply naïve, pre-critical – that is, pre-Kantian – thinkers who, in alluding to a subtle body, were actually alluding to a psychological process, not a literal, somatic, alchemical one. But the alchemists like Dorn were in fact using metallurgical symbols both to communicate a literal somatic transmutation to initiates and give the impression of writing about the transmutation of metals to those outside the alchemical tradition.

Thus traditional schools of alchemy, like other esoteric traditions in the West, continued the ancient practice of creating and maintaining conditions of inner development for those called to such a way of life. And in all these traditions the proper attitude toward thought was maintained: the valuation not of the content of thought, ordinary thought, but of Thought itself, Awareness itself, Being itself.

Western Religious or Theological Thought

Western theology and religious studies have by and large capitulated to modern science and philosophy. Ancient Western religious thought was highly influenced by Platonic categories, medieval religious thought by Aristotelian categories. Thus the history of Western religion and theology has always tended to follow the dominant currents of thought of the holding culture. Only in the High Middle Ages, when the Church was indeed triumphant, did theological thought dominate a Western landscape.

The teaching of theology and religious studies in our universities, even those associated with religious institutions, faithfully track the holding culture in its scientific and scholarly approach to knowledge. Once more one encounters the primacy of the content of thought: the whole purpose of scholarship and education is to arrive at correct opinions, to the degree possible. Any suggestion that such study should assist one to develop being would be met with lifted brows and agog jaws.

Biblical studies provide a good example of this phenomenon. Several events transpired in Western thinking that have yielded a vast expenditure of energy over a relatively unimportant set of questions concerning the sacred scripture of Jews and Christians that we call the Bible. The first in order came primarily in German universities, where the Bible began to be examined from a "scientific" or scholarly point of view rather than a devotional viewpoint. Different forms of "criticism" were developed: textual, form, redaction, and so on. Conclusions drawn on the basis of these critiques, no matter how tentative, were deeply disturbing to those clergy and laity, particularly in English speaking countries, who held to the verbal inspiration of the Bible. The idea that a letter of Paul was not really written by Paul, or that the gospel of Mark was likely written by a much later author, was not readily received. And worse revelations awaited those who accepted the Bible's account of historical events as true. Eventually seminaries and universities in England and the United States succumbed to this "higher criticism," much to the chagrin of fundamentalist and evangelical Christians along with orthodox Jews. Soon enough those seminary students who accepted such critical views became leaders and pastors of churches or themselves became professors, continuing the legacy begun in Germany in the 19th century. And one result of all this conflict has been a slow but steady decline in the faithful attendance of more liberal churches while the more conservative churches have been holding relatively steady while fighting a rearguard action.

Now all this conflict, all this expenditure of excessive heat with precious little light, is a conflict over opinion, not knowledge or truth. Whether Paul really wrote Romans, or whether one holds a correct set of beliefs based upon that letter, is not only relatively trivial and unimportant but is also a typical example of how the content of thought works to blind us to the important questions of life.

Debates regarding theological questions have this same property: they assume an altogether unworthy importance in the minds of those who believe that correct opinions are necessary – even, so some maintain, to salvation, whatever that might mean. But it is usually this concern with the salvation of oneself and others that places such an undue stress upon correct beliefs or opinions about this or that doctrine.

Undue concern about doctrine is also the source of most if not all of the religious violence that has so plagued and continues to plague our embattled world. In the history of Christian thought, for example, the Spanish Inquisition served to bring recalcitrant heretics into doctrinal line. And concern for one's own salvation and the salvation of others can lead power possessors to inflict torture and even death upon those who do not wish to be saved. And evidently the touchstone for salvation is not Being or the lack thereof but "sound doctrine" or belief.

Western Contemplative Thought

In contrast to this Western obsession with the content of thought is the history of Western, often Christian, contemplative thought, some of it a product of esoteric schools like alchemy, but some issuing from more traditional Christian settings, primarily the monasteries of the Catholic Church.

Although most monastics and hermits are orthodox in their belief and hold "sound" doctrines, the content of their thought does not assume the ultimate concern of their lives or their thought life. What assumes primary importance is a set of spiritual disciplines or practices intended to develop being, primarily devotional feeling, in an effort to attain union with God. In this regard their monastic settings are more like ancient spiritual schools than the universities and seminaries of modern and postmodern times.

The tenor of modern and postmodern contemplative thought was set by Abbot Thomas Keating, now at Snowmass monastery in Colorado, and chief advocate for what has become known as Contemplative Outreach. This program, created in a monastic setting, reaches out to those not in such settings as a way of introducing a way of life concerned primarily with the development of being as the only way to "rest" in God and ultimately attain union with the higher. More specifically it involves being instructed in the sort of seated meditation practiced in spiritual schools worldwide and learning a "prayer word" to be repeated as a sort of mantra until one begins to discover the silence of authentic contemplative prayer. Here prayer is conceived not as petition but as contemplation, in silence.

With this movement, and with others like it, we come full circle in Western thought. Aristotle maintained that the highest thought is contemplation, and in that he echoed the teaching of Socrates and Plato that only a quiet mind, a silent mind, can receive Being and Energy from above. And in a later chapter we will examine the most significant spiritual teaching of our day, delivered by an Eastern master who came to the West to bring a teaching meant first for the West, and eventually for the East as well. In that teaching, too, contemplation is the highest form of thought.

CHAPTER FOUR

EASTERN THOUGHT

The Distinctive Nature of Eastern Thought

Eastern thought, unlike Western thought, never counted the *content* of thought, correct opinion or belief, as the truth of reality or Being. Rather, Eastern thought has consistently maintained that attainment of Truth can only obtain as a result of a growing development both of certainty and being.

Eastern thought cannot be easily summarized aside from the above statements. Yet despite the differences that appear in the cultures and climates that comprise the East, an overarching concern with becoming and being, development and certainty, is clearly discerned. In the East, ordinary thought or reason was critiqued as thoroughly as in the West, yet the pervasive resignation so characteristic of the West never dominated Eastern thinking; instead, various remedies were offered, remedies that promised an eventual liberation of thought.

Advaita Vedanta

The schools of thought in the East are so vast in number that it is necessary to be selective in considering examples. In the Indian subcontinent alone many interesting schools of thought offer remedies to thought's enslavement to desire. Probably the school that has most influenced the thinking of the West in modern and postmodern times is that of Advaita Vedanta.

Vedanta means the end of the Vedas, and the Vedas are scriptures that give us some idea of the ancient sacrificial religious system of the Aryans. Advaita means not-two or nondual, so the school of Advaita Vedanta begins with the idea that reality is nondual. This striking and usually counterintuitive guiding idea is not intended to be defended as a doctrine; rather, its purpose is to help guide a school aspirant to the truth of Being. Appearances notwithstanding, we are not separate beings but one Being, the great Self, Atman, or Brahman. What this suggests is that our apparently separate faculties of reason and desire are manifestations of, and unfortunately also veil, our authentic Identity.

If our real Identity is so veiled by more surface manifestations, then the first order of business is to attain the development of being needed to discriminate among the differing levels in our inner structure. In so doing, we also come to discriminate between ordinary thought ruled by the desires of an ersatz self and the Objective Thought of our real Self. We also learn to discriminate among desires: desires that only distantly and distortedly reflect our real needs, and desires that more faithfully reflect need.

Vedanta is a tradition that places emphasis upon the attainment of knowledge by the use of the intellect. This emphasis means that the tradition has a way of teaching that creates the right conditions for a gradual growth or development of being. Absent actual experience in a school of being, this emphasis upon knowledge and the intellect might suggest an intellectual development only; however, this tradition also touches and develops the feeling and somatic centers of intelligence as well. First, however, certain intellectual attitudes and beliefs must be challenged, and that is why Vedanta begins with the intellect and with sacred ideas meant to overturn societal conditioning.

As with all the other Eastern traditions that seek to liberate thought, Thought itself, Being itself, is invoked to end an exclusive reliance upon thought. For only by so doing can thought be liberated and reality known.

Tibetan Buddhism

Tibetan or Vajrayana Buddhism is a synthesis of indigenous Tibetan traditions like Bon and Buddhist teaching imported from India. The Dalai Lama maintains that it is the most complete form of Buddhism, incorporating Hinayana, Mahayana, and of course Vajrayana. It is also the form of Buddhism that most utilizes the Eastern practices of Tantra, with an emphasis upon inner energies and the development of the subtle or radiant body.

The Buddha's original teaching maintained that only by a withdrawal of attachment to a false identity along with its desires can one be liberated or enlightened. All Tibetan practices are intended to advance that liberation, and the liberation of thought from illusory desires is an essential part of that awakening. All ordinary thought is in service to desire, and such desire is created and sustained by a mistaken identity; once this identity is recognized as mistaken, the natural process of development is in the direction of a withdrawal of emotional energy from this ersatz feeling of self and its desires.

Tantric teaching, which is not confined to any one Eastern school of thought, helps an aspirant discriminate among the inner energies of thought, feeling, sensation, along with initiating the reception of higher energy along the vertical axis of the body. Development of being, and the concomitant realization of certainty, depends upon this reception, and the transmission of subtle energies from teacher, master, or guru to disciple or aspirant is considered mandatory. Hence the emphasis upon guru yoga in this tradition, an emphasis that also obtains in many other Eastern schools of development.

Work with a guru is seen as an intermediate phase of development, between the usual, soporific state of being and the eventual Self-realization. Yoga indicates not only a yoking or attachment to something but also an unyoking to something else: an abandonment of the usual identification with a false sense of self and an adoption of a temporary identification with the guru, who represents the Self one really is. Over time, this identification is also abandoned as one recognizes and in effect becomes one's authentic Being.

Gurus and Schools

The practice of guru yoga, virtually uniform in the traditional East, is not incompatible with the school conditions already discussed, and in fact an authentic guru of necessity must gather about him a community of devotees, necessary because there is little time for exclusive one-on-one master to disciple instruction.

So because of this necessity, school conditions are established that help regulate both guru and devotees, while simultaneously reorienting aspirants from what can even in the East be called a psychological mindset to an energetic orientation, from social and familial conditioning to a growing familiarity with the energetic foundation of reality itself. And an essential part of this gradual turn toward the real and away from the societal veneer is a growing disenchantment with the conceptual mind and its futile effort to represent the real in words.

Taoism

No Eastern school of thought is more emblematic of this turn from concepts to energy than Taoism, born in China and assuming its ultimate literary form in Lao Tze's classic *Tao Teh Ching*. In that work words are used beautifully to seduce us from words.

The Tao, or Reality, that can be spoken or represented in concepts is not the real Tao – so this classic text tells us. And the noblest human attributes which are aligned with the Tao are also beyond the power of ordinary thought to represent: authentic virtue, for example, cannot be attained using a conceptual ideal. The most lofty idea of all – *wu wei* or letting be – warns against a wrongheaded attempt to use the conceptual, ordinary mind or reason to storm the gates of heaven. Instead, letting things be as they are illustrates the receptive mindset needed to abandon one's societal "will" in order to invite the descent and embodiment of authentic Will. This Will is real Thought, free from societal influence, familial conditioning, the false self, and the process of desire.

Zen

More familiar to the West is the form of Buddhism known as Zen, born also in China as Chan Buddhism, a synthesis of Mahayana Buddhism from India and the indigenous Taoist tradition. Though born in China, this form of Buddhism became known best in Western countries in its distinctive Japanese forms, particularly Rinzai and Soto.

Although much interest has always been generated in the West toward Rinzai Zen with its koans or riddles intended to challenge and decisively frustrate the conceptual mind, Soto Zen offers only one riddle, that of just sitting. In a Soto school or community, such as that which was established in San Francisco, the community of aspirants are given talks by the master and then told to "just sit." And it is this just sitting that most exemplifies the liberated state of a Buddha.

Of course with this teaching and the demand to sit for hours on end the ordinary mind is frustrated no end. As in the Rinzai school, the usual rationality that blindly serves desires for special outcomes is rendered useless; during a sitting the mind may race furiously in a mad attempt to figure things out. Yet the instruction is to attend all such futile thought with real Thought, with a higher Attention or Awareness that is the Buddha-mind.

To ask how can just sitting issue in authentic change or transformation is to ask how being can possibly spark becoming. Higher being penetrates into lower being to create intermediate being, or, as Gurdjieff put it, the higher blends with the lower to actualize the middle. Thus becoming, the creation of a higher level of being, is produced by the interaction of different levels of being. The usual feeling of self, the lower being-level, is surrendered into the divine life-current, the feeling of Being itself in the body-mind structure.

Eastern Christianity

A remarkable document of the Eastern Orthodox Church called the *Philokalia* records the efforts of monks and anchorites to submit to this higher level of being, all within the context of orthodox Christian teaching. Unlike most Western Christian writings, the Eastern Christian spiritual schools associated prayer with the development of attention and higher being.

These ascetics understood that authentic prayer was not possible without help from above. Real prayer was not something a man or woman could do, unless he or she was willing to sacrifice his or her own "will" into a current of energy descending from above the head. Eastern Christian thought often wrote about the "energies of God," and submission to these energies was required before prayer could become a possibility.

Above all the development of being is a development of feeling, feeling as an organ of knowledge or understanding, and Eastern thought, cutting across all the religious and spiritual traditions of the East, teaches that devotion to the Higher, to the Beloved, must be cultivated; the Beloved must be wooed as one woos a lover. One must fall in love with Being in order to be transformed from above.

Although these ascetics were orthodox in belief, concerns with doctrine, the content of thought, were far from occupying a central part of their attention. Instead, and in dramatic contrast to the vast majority of their fellow Christians, their primary concern was in embodying the received tradition by opening to and receiving the energies of God, understanding that only by so doing would they be able to be Christians in fact and not in name only. And the emphasis was in being *able* to be Christians.

Sufi Schools

Islamic schools of thought, particularly the more esoteric, belong grouped together with the other Eastern schools, not the Western. Islam, born in the Arabian peninsula, and despite its expansion by conquest into the West, remains centered in the Middle East.

Islam, like the other monotheistic religions that place considerable importance upon their historical origins, has reacted to the increasingly secular thought of the West by becoming more concerned about its doctrine. Christianity and Judaism have also reacted similarly, the former by emphasizing dogma and doctrine, the latter by conforming to the Western secular culture. For this reason in all three religions a primary interest in the development of being or Thought itself places an interest in the content of thought, or doctrine, as a secondary concern, and is by and large confined to esoteric schools of thought.

Sufi schools comprise the esoteric dimension of Islam, and, using various spiritual exercises and disciplines such as movement or sacred dance and attempts to "remember" God, ordinary thought, even doctrinal thought, is sacrificed for the sake of a submission of the entire body-mind to Thought itself, Attention itself, to the current or energy of God.

Unlike most other Eastern schools, Sufi schools do not enjoy much support from the surrounding culture. In this respect they face the same difficulties as the more esoteric currents of Christianity and Judaism. The difficulty is due to a fundamentalist reaction of the larger religion to the inroads of modern and postmodern secular Western culture into more traditional ways of living and thinking. This understandable reaction has had the unfortunate effect of placing even more emphasis on the content of thought to the increasing neglect of a recognition of Thought itself. Those called to this sacred search for Being must conduct it in schools apart from the holding religious culture – hence the need for secrecy, for an esoteric understanding not only of Thought but also the holding tradition or religion.

It may also appear that Islam is a decisive counterexample to the idea that Eastern thought never counted the content of thought as the truth or reality of

Being. If true, Islam shares this feature with Judaism and Christianity, both born in the Middle East and both reacting strongly to modern Western culture. This truth, however, applies only to the exoteric forms of these three religions. To be sure, the exoteric form of each represents the outer, doctrinal teaching, conditioned by their historical interest in the genesis and development of their tradition. But the authentic form of each remains the inner, esoteric practices that lead an aspirant to the real Truth of the faith. Hence Sufism is not only the heart of Islam but also shares with Eastern thought in general its abiding interest in Thought or Being itself. The preoccupation with the content of its religious thought Islam shares with the two religions which, though born in the East, have found a congenial home in the West.

Yogas

We have already seen how guru yoga helps to define Eastern schools; what we have yet to consider is how different forms of yoga address different parts of the human being, appealing to different types of individuals who may be drawn to one or the other forms of yoga or spiritual discipline in order to attain Self-realization and continue ontological development.

Raja yoga and jnana yoga, like Advaita Vedanta, address those of an "intellectual" bent – not, however, by cultivating intellectual interests in thought-content or the conceptual mind but by starting there and moving on to other, equally important dimensions of human nature.

Hatha yoga, a degenerate form of which is familiar in the West, addresses the body and prepares it for the reception of higher energy or Thought. Some ascetics or fakirs in India try to storm heaven's gates by enduring the most taxing of physical disciplines, holding an arm up until it ceases to function as a limb and becomes a virtual stick, for example. More moderate forms of hatha yoga prepare the central nervous system for the eventual creation of a second or subtle body.

Karma yoga addresses those more involved in the world as the yoga of inaction in action, or action in inaction. Depending as it does on the notion of karma, this form of yoga teaches aspirants that no further karma or consequences of actions will be created if the yogin acts without attachment to any preferred outcome. By this practice or discipline the habit of entertaining egoic desires and acting on them is undermined rather than undergirded, as it is with habitual, conditioned actions.

Bhakti yoga addresses those attracted to spiritual disciplines that use devotion as a direct way to abandon egoic desire and develop feeling for one's guru and, through him, the Beloved, Being itself.

All of these differing forms of yoga wind up addressing the whole human structure in an attempt to provide the aspirant a second education about what it means to be human; the differences among them involve not where one winds up, but from which vantage point one starts.

The Upanishads

If any form of extant Eastern literature might tempt one to conclude that the East has an equally vibrant concern with the content of thought as the West, it would be the Upanishads. The very name translates as something like seminars in English, suggesting an academic approach to thought; however, even a cursory examination of this literature at once dispels this suggestion.

The structure of the material is in the form of dialogues among disciples and a teacher or master, and most often treats the obstacles that prevent a direct recognition and reception of the higher energy of Truth. Ordinary thought, as utilized in academic seminars for example, is quickly dismissed as an impediment to a realization of the real. What is emphasized instead is Thought itself, what many traditions call the Witness, a higher Attention or Awareness that simply watches without judgment, accepts everything, and which the aspirant comes to recognize as the divine condition itself as well as one's authentic Identity.

The Upanishads figure importantly in the continuing tradition of Advaita Vedanta, that form of Eastern thought that has most influenced the West. Yet here too, in the West, Vedantic teachings assume importance as doctrines, not as sacred ideas designed to convey one beyond doctrine, beyond ordinary thought or opinion. The most difficult hurdle for any Eastern way of life or thought is to overcome the well-ingrained Western habit of placing primary importance upon correct opinion or belief. The very identity that the Upanishads tries to uproot is inextricably tangled in the toxic outgrowth of doctrine, of belief.

The Influence of Western Thought

Just as Eastern thought has penetrated and influenced the West, so Western thought has penetrated and influenced the East, the former in ways that make more accessible alternative ways of living and being, the latter that make less attractive traditional Eastern ways of discovery and development.

The influence of Western thought is by and large baneful, in that it makes more attractive to the Eastern mind the pervasive resignation so characteristic of the West, the same resignation that has convinced most Western thinkers that the real cannot be known. Thus Easterners exposed to Western thought, and especially those educated in the West, find such resignation both more accessible and more convincing than the remedies offered in the East: more accessible, because all that is demanded is a belief or conviction assumed by the isolated intellect; more convincing, in that it is the philosophy of existence of the holding culture within which one is educated and to which one wishes to conform. The more demanding ways of life that comprise the disciplines and schools of the varied Eastern remedies are not only far less accessible but are also far less attractive.

Yet the most potent form of spiritual teaching with its concomitant school both for native Westerners and for Easterners influenced by the West was born in the East, and, eventually, taught primarily in the West. And it is this teaching and this school that more than any other has reignited an interest in the necessity of school conditions for the attainment of Being and truth. We will examine this school in the next chapter.

CHAPTER FIVE

GURDJIEFF AND HIS SCHOOL

Ecce Homo

Gurdjieff the man is an enigma, an unknown spiritual force who emerged from an unknown past and remained an unknown figure even to those closest to him. A consummate role-player, a master of masks and disguises, he nevertheless brought a teaching so clear and decisive that it has taken the lead among teachings that now compete for the minds and hearts of Western, postmodern men and women. The fuller establishment of the school itself had to await his death, and, as Nietzsche once observed, some are born posthumously. Gurdjieff is such a one.

As master of disguises, Gurdjieff created both himself and his past for his followers and for the public at large. He did this primarily in his second series of writings, *Meetings with Remarkable Men*. In that book he presents himself as one who, with others, was in search of truth and journeyed to "inaccessible places" in quest of greater being. As the story unfolds we find the young Gurdjieff eventually discovering the truth in a remote monastery of seekers called the Sarmoung brotherhood. He is advised by his mentor to remain there until he attains a "force" in him which "nothing can destroy." Then, so the advice continues, he can leave the school of work to take what he has learned to others.

The next portion of Gurdjieff's life is best captured in P.D. Ouspensky's *In Search of the Miraculous*. In that work we learn that Gurdjieff had begun his teaching career in pre-Soviet Russia, in St. Petersburg and Moscow. Ouspensky also outlines his "fragments of an unknown teaching" but provides a compelling picture of the man Gurdjieff as well. We are confronted with an articulate, educated, intelligent, compassionate man who is able to challenge lifelong conditioning with sacred ideas. In addition, it is obvious that he needs no help in "stepping down" this teaching so others can understand; he knows that the presented ideas must be supported with lived experience.

Other books by other students of Gurdjieff supply more information about his post-Russia experiences and the man himself. Gurdjieff and his followers had to flee Russia as the Bolshevik revolution was underway. They fled across the Caucasus to Constantinople, and from there to a chateau in Fountainbleau near Paris called the Prieure. There Gurdjieff established the first formal school conditions that made possible the effective transmission of his teaching. We will examine these conditions along with the teaching later in this chapter. But first more about the man.

In the midst of this activity Gurdjieff suffered a near fatal car accident. After his slow recovery, he closed the school and decided to devote his remaining time to writing. He wrote three series of books: the first, *Beelzebub's Tales to His Grandson*, was intended for the world at large, and was also intended to be read aloud, and indeed in so reading assumed the form of an ancient bardic tale; the second we have already mentioned, *Meetings with Remarkable Men*; the third, unfinished, *Life Is Real Only Then, When I Am*, was intended for experienced students of the school with enough depth to understand its more esoteric ideas.

Although the school had been formally closed, and Gurdjieff was occupied with writing, he continued to guide students along the way of his teaching. He eventually moved to a small apartment in Paris, and remained there during the Nazi occupation, secretly holding evening gatherings and preparing meals for the many guests who would arrive, mostly comprised of his pupils. Where possible, he also assisted those in need, purchasing art, distributing candies to children, and in many such ways demonstrating his concern also for those who were not among his followers.

During the last years of his life Gurdjieff wanted to ensure the continuation of his ideas, and so worked individually with the more elder students who would assume that responsibility. He thought not only of Paris and France but also was interested in groups in London and especially the group in New York, led by the famous editor and thinker Alfred Orage. With Orage's death Gurdjieff selected John Sinclair, Lord Pentland, to head the New York group. Over the years Gurdjieff had made several ocean voyages to the United States, bringing his movements and dances, and thought his work would flourish best in the New World.

Gurdjieff collapsed when leading a movements class, and died soon thereafter. He entrusted his work to Jeanne de Salzmann, and it was she who established the most formal conditions for a school of inner work.

Gurdjieff's Sacred Ideas

Several written sources exist to explore the sacred ideas Gurdjieff left the world and which his school teaches to this day. Perhaps the most accessible is Ouspensky's classic account *In Search of the Miraculous*; more difficult of access is Gurdjieff's own *Beelzebub's Tales*, usually read aloud by members of the groups that exist in almost every large city; an essay by Jacob Needleman, "Gurdjieff and His School," is a good introduction, and appears in a volume of essays called *Modern Esoteric Spirituality*; the notebooks of Jeanne de Salzmann have been assembled by her family and work-friends into a book, *The Reality of Being*, which is well worth reading but, like Gurdjieff's *Life is Real*, can be understood only with sufficient experience and is therefore best confined to those with considerable exposure to school conditions.

According to Gurdjieff, and in agreement with other sacred teachings, men and women are asleep to their own reality. They are conditioned to accept the identities inculcated by family and society at large as their authentic selves, and grow up to endure this pinched self-sense despite the heartache and suffering it causes. Given a developed and relatively free society, varied respites from this suffering are offered, some in the form of entertainment, high and low, others in the form of addictions, compulsions, and other self-destructive activities. During the 20th century, as Gurdjieff was formulating and then presenting his ideas, there also appeared therapeutic measures designed not only to provide some relief from emotional and mental distress but also meant to challenge one's usual picture or view of oneself and offer a more realistic view, one that would comport better with the holding culture.

The basic idea here, as articulated best by Freud, is that individual desires and cultural demands are at loggerheads. Therapeutic psychology, then, intended to ameliorate this conflict, not remove it, for Freud taught that desire and societal restraint could never come to a satisfying resolution. Gurdjieff knew enough about this approach to understand that, though helpful in many cases in providing some relief, it failed to comprehend the more primordial processes that set men and women up for ongoing conflict and distress. Above all, it assumed that there already existed in the human frame sufficient unity and continuity upon which to erect a therapeutic scaffolding that could in turn be used to alter the façade of the building. In addressing this mistaken assumption we can also address one of Gurdjieff's most central ideas.

Fragmentation

The idea, as Gurdjieff taught, that challenges the efficacy and indeed therapeutic nature of psychoanalysis and other psychological approaches to mental and emotional wellness is that human beings are fragmented to such a degree that neither unity nor continuity is possible without a radical reorientation in the midst of a spiritual school. And unless this fragmentation is clearly seen we will continue to entertain a collection of conceits about who we are and what we can do.

This state of fragmentation also accounts for our conflicting desires and the resultant inner contradictions among desires. One part of ourselves wants one thing, while another part wants something quite different, often a polar opposite. People in the recovery movement – those who band together to help one another abstain from various dysfunctional addictions – are familiar with this phenomenon. One fragment, one 'I', wants to drink or use drugs, while another fragment, another 'I', wants to abstain from such activities. Inevitably, the strongest desire wins, and the part that loses will punish the part that has won. And all the nonsense about "will power" will also enter the fray to complicate further the struggle to stay "clean and sober." This drama will continue to play out until an individual understands fragmentation.

Step one in the 12 step program of AA, Alcoholics Anonymous, is a confession of powerlessness and also a confession of belief in a higher source of power one can access to find help. What is the cause of this powerlessness? And what is this "higher power"?

Our power is our energy, our feeling of Self, our attention, and the cause of our powerlessness in the face of conflicting desires, in capitulating to desires that work against our well-being, is the unconscious and habitual surrender of our power, our attention, our very identity, to the strongest desire. The cause of powerlessness is the *process* of desire, the process of surrendering our power to a lower force.

We need to see, through direct experience, how our power can be restored – not by continuing a futile struggle on the lower level where attention is captured, fragmentation obtains, and our identity shifts from wishing one thing one moment to wishing another in the next moment, but rather by learning how attention, our energy, our power, our very identity, first has the power to step back from the ordinary mind with its contradictory desires and enslaved thought, to refine its own energy, to rise above the conflict and simply watch, without judgment or comment, the forces that perpetuate the conflict.

Who am I? I am attention, and attention has many levels and qualities, many stages of refinement. Where am I, then, in this feeling of powerlessness? I am lost in a battle of conflicting desires, in which I identify with both sides of a given conflict, now with this desire, now with its antagonist. I have forgotten myself, forgotten attention, forgotten its power to refine itself and rise above the struggle, forgotten my only source of help. In religious language, my help comes from the Lord.

So I need to remember myself, remember who I am, remember where my power lies, remember my identity as attention with its power to connect two worlds, the lower world of conflicting desires and the higher world of power and help. Above all I need to *see*, in the moment of struggle below, where my power of free will, free choice, resides, and in that seeing understand what it means to "act like a man," to understand the real meaning of human action in the lower world, how to allow finer, higher energies to penetrate the very tissues of the body.

Where am I, then, in this *confession* of powerlessness and in the concomitant recognition of a need for higher help? In the moment of confession I am already a little freer, my attention is already a little more refined – *but it is most important to recognize this fact*, for without this recognition I will immediately return to my usual, ordinary state of enslaved attention: one moment identified with one desire, the next with another, one moment wishing to recover from an addiction, the next moment wishing to indulge it. By recognizing the real source of my power – attention or awareness – I am able to rise above the conflict entirely and, in that moment, *empower* the wish to take appropriate action for my well-being on all levels, higher and lower. And, given time with its repeated return to an awareness of attention in the moment, more consistently favor those desires that faithfully reflect authentic need, most especially the *need for Being*, the need to *recognize* attention as 'I' and allow this *feeling* of 'I' to develop. As always, discovery and an ongoing development work together for our highest good.

There is empowerment available to those struggling with addictions in 12 step groups, partly because those who attend experience moments of a freer attention, a feeling of 'I am' and 'I can do.' And, along with the shared experiences of strength and hope, this feeling is what keeps people returning to the meetings. Yet outside of the meetings people remain vulnerable to their usual, restricted, identified feeling of 'I', and thus prey to the strongest desire. Sometimes, because of the empowerment received at a meeting, the desire to recover from the addiction wins; sometimes the desire to indulge the addiction wins. It is strictly a question of the forces operating on this lower level because, in that moment, no understanding of how to access one's power to help is available. Such an understanding constitutes authentic "will power."

Conditions for True Action

Another important idea, one that relates to the therapeutic attempt to remedy distress, is that we cannot engage in true action, cannot "do" anything, in our fragmented state. Because we are asleep to our real condition, and do not understand our conditioning, we cannot see that our actions are not free but driven by inner motivations and outer conditions – driven, primarily, by desire.

Therapeutic psychology itself teaches that our actions are determined by our motivations, by our desires, and that any change in our behavior depends upon a change in the determining conditions that drive our actions. The question of whether any of these conditions or possible changes constitute freedom in any meaningful sense of the term is rarely addressed, and if it is, freedom is usually affirmed even in the teeth of the indispensable determining factor of motivations. Gurdjieff taught that the ability to entertain this contradiction is a measure of our ignorance of the fundamental existential predicament we face.

The freedom we may be able to exercise lies not in our supposed ability to augment one desire over another, to exercise "will power." Put simply, our potential freedom lies in the conscious exercise of our attention, to attend one thing rather than another, and especially *to attend attention itself.*

The life of desire, of motivation, favoring one desire over another in cases of conflicting motives, for example, is a life of *conditioning*, a life within which, absent authentic consciousness, we deceive ourselves into believing we have free choice. In cases of conflicting desires or motives, the strongest desire always wins. But we can never directly augment one desire over another, even when we believe it is a better alternative. To attempt to do so is to attempt to alter the strength of one desire with the opposing or conflicting desire, to change one part of the mind with another part, both on the same level of being. We can only exercise influence indirectly by *understanding* the automaticity of our conditioning and the real Source of our help and freedom.

Real help and freedom come from above, not from our conditioning. And all the virtues and finer qualities we try futilely to cultivate or generate on our own level are only available in a higher consciousness, virtues like patience, acceptance, fortitude, service, love. The power to transform our lives, to act with compassion toward ourselves and others, comes from a higher attention or awareness that literally penetrates into the tissues of our bodies, where tensions hold in place the implacable societal conditioning that decisively determines our lower motivations: fear, anger, resentment, impatience, egoism.

True action, according to Gurdjieff, is dependent upon a free act or movement anterior to the manifestation that we usually dub "action." Primordial action is a movement of the attention, even the most modest, which can include choosing to attend this object rather than another. This anterior action of attention must become an object of interest and study before any further steps toward unity and continuity, toward real "doing," can occur.

The Movement Toward Unity

How to move from fragmentation toward unity? First the attention must be recognized as our only source not only of freedom but also of identity. And because desires, or motivations, support an altogether mistaken sense of identity, the process of desire or identification itself must be questioned. And the most difficult challenge in the study of attention is to come to an understanding of an attention without motivation.

Psychology teaches that actions are driven by motivations, by desires. Gurdjieff taught that our fragmentation, and our mistaken, incomplete sense and feeling of self, is driven by desires. Thus if there is any possible freedom in the human being it must be a freedom from motivation, from desire, and in this freedom lies another possible freedom: freedom to create a bridge from fragmentation to unity.

So long as motivations are considered essential to being human, so long will human beings fall short of being human, fall short of Being itself. Psychology insists that they are essential, and in that insistence it fails to grasp the most fundamental existential predicament and also perpetuates it. The motivational life of fragmentation offers no possible way from here to There, from a state of dissociation to a state of Unity. The very science that claims to understand how the mind works fails to understand the mind's working.

The Study of Attention

Gurdjieff highlighted the study of attention, its levels and qualities. For in this study lies the freedom from motivations, from desires, and from the process of desire itself, the process of identification.

Of course spiritual teachings must be sly: one must be tricked out of the life of motivation, just as one was tricked into it by the holding culture. And once again, for this process a community, a school, of likeminded individuals is mandatory. The conditioning we have all absorbed is too bound up with our most cherished beliefs about ourselves to be successfully challenged without help from the conditions created by those who have themselves been weaned from cultural hegemony. They must be sly because we all enter even the most favorable spiritual conditions with the most intractable of convictions: the conceited assurance that we are who we think we are and that we can do what we believe we can do. Both convictions are false.

These convictions are founded upon the conceptual mind, in turn created and supported by the process of desire, which, in concert with the mind, supports the ongoing sense of mistaken identity. Gurdjieff's teaching about the priority of attention prepares the way for an inclusion of other intelligences, other attentions, than the conceptual intelligence with which we are most familiar.

Centers of Intelligence

In the Gurdjieff school the attention with which we are most familiar is used to begin a study of other centers of intelligence: the body, with its instincts and movements, and the feeling. In addition to the three lower centers of the mind, feeling, and body, students are taught there are two higher centers, one emotional and the other intellectual. But at first primary interest is in the study of the two centers, body and feeling, with which most individuals are not familiar.

Soon after this study is commenced, another idea is introduced: that the movement from fragmentation to unity cannot occur without a movement of attention from the mind to the body. In our usual fragmented state the attention of the mind is occupied with drifting, daydreams, fantasies, or perhaps with some attractive object or desire, while the body is left to itself, unattended; the body may interrupt a given daydream or fantasy with an itch, ache, or other bid for attention, but usually it is forgotten. Gurdjieff insists that it be remembered, and that the attention normally given over to the pursuit of egoic desire or just aimless drifting be directed into the tissues of the body, there to discover an inner sensation of self, a Presence, about which one was unaware except for brief periods, particularly in childhood, but concerning which one did not have the needed ideas to understand, much less value, its appearance.

So begins a serious study of sensation, at first a sensation of the body, later a sensation of oneself in the body, a sensation, a feeling, of Presence, which Gurdjieff named Self-remembering. The sensation of the body, and the sensation of oneself in the body – a sense and feeling of embodiment – is the sign that the mind and the body are connected, and this connection is the initiation of a process of movement toward unity, toward wholeness of being and action.

I Am Here, I Can Do

The sensation and feeling of Presence is a feeling of 'I am,' a feeling of Being, and, as this feeling indicates, the joining of the mind and the body calls the third lower center, the feeling, to participate in the direct understanding of the reality of Being itself. It is a feeling of "I am here" and "I can do." Gurdjieff taught that with sufficient unity one could both *be* and *do*; in his words, "do the work of a real man."

Given sufficient unity of mind, body, and feeling, the study of attention proceeds to include an even finer attention or energy from another level, the level of the higher feeling center. The work of a "real man" includes the necessity of opening to this higher level, for without this submission no further ontological development is possible. A certain development of being is needed to open at all, and this development occurs during the initial stages of work with Gurdjieff's school. For further development to occur, higher being or energy must be received in the tissues of the body from two sources: active elements of air, via the breath, and impressions received consciously, via Presence. The developing sense and feeling of Presence in the body is fed from these two sources.

Shakti

Many Eastern traditions are familiar with the being-creating workings of *Shakti* or *prana*, names given to the higher emotional energy that enters the vertical axis of the body from above the head. Unfortunately there are many degenerate traditions that speak of *kundalini* as the transformative energy, but not only is it a manifestation of uncontrolled sexual energy but it also serves to obstruct the authentic movement of energy from above downwards by its opposing movement up the spine toward the crown of the head. Gurdjieff was especially insistent that the authentic transformative force not be confused with the *kundalini* phenomenon that has prevented the further development of so many seekers.

Gurdjieff instituted "sittings" with specially prepared, elder pupils for the purpose of introducing the reception of the higher emotional force. After his death, his star pupil, Jeanne de Salzmann, eventually widened the practice of sittings in groups while speaking more openly of the reception of *prana,* the force needed to complete the creation of a subtle body or organism, the next step in the ontological evolution of the human being and an essential part of the eventual discovery and ongoing recognition of one's authentic Identity. It was also Jeanne de Salzmann who established the currently extant school conditions that obtain in the Gurdjieff line of work.

School Conditions

Any discussion of the conditions for the absorption of the sacred ideas introduced into the West by Gurdjieff must include his decision that for Westerners self-initiation would be better served in a group setting than in the guru setting so characteristic of Eastern schools.

This decision has proven to be especially prescient given the many tribulations that have been encountered in attempts to transplant Eastern traditions with their cultural trappings into the West with its more radical individualism and suspicion of authority. To take only one example, many female seekers have claimed abuse from male gurus or masters; the claim is usually that the master taught that sexual involvement would issue in ontological development but that the primary interest was in sating the master's own desires. Be that as it may, this phenomenon, which has been repeated across transplanted traditions in the West, serves as an indicator that perhaps the guru-devotee tradition of discovery and development is not optimal for Western seekers.

In addition, the Gurdjieff conditions of group work has had a profound and lasting impact upon psychotherapeutic protocols which began on the West coast in the humanistic center called Esalen: the encounter group, the marathon group, the psychodrama group, all such attempts to provide psychological services to people were inspired by the idea of group work in the Gurdjieff school. In the humanistic or third-force school of psychology, emphasis was placed more on "growth" and "self-actualization" than on the "working through" of psychodynamic approaches and the thought "restructuring" and behavior "modification" of the cognitive-behavioral approaches. The dynamic of group work in the Gurdjieff school that facilitated sincere exchanges with peers and elders was thought to be applicable to exchanges in psychological "growth" settings also. The San Francisco group led by John Pentland was the chief source of inspiration.

Movements and Dances

Gurdjieff described himself as a "teacher of dancing," and was especially interested in the study of movement and dancing as a way to experience the movement toward unity. The movements and dances introduced by Gurdjieff and carried forward by his pupils was literally a way to move from fragmentation to unity.

This movement occurred in two ways: first, and most apparent, was the movement toward unity in the moment of executing the movements; second was the growing ability to inhabit the body during movement, an ability acquired over time.

Such movements or dances have the property of unifying the three lower centers of intelligence and can even invite the descent of higher emotional energy. The mind or head brain concentrates on the execution of the movement, which of course demands attention to the body, and, with the music, the feeling is called as well. Combining the three in this compelling manner invites help from above.

Music

In addition to the music created for the movements, Gurdjieff collaborated with gifted composer Thomas de Hartmann to create an extraordinary body of listening music that has a profoundly emotional effect on all who listen with open mind, body, and heart. For those who have listened, or played, this music over a certain period of time, it is discovered that each piece, usually played on a piano, evokes the same feeling and somatic sensations with every performance, suggesting strongly an objective intention in its creation.

An interesting variation to the music is performed with great effect in Peter Brook's film *Meetings with Remarkable Men*, based on Gurdjieff's book. In addition, the first filmed public presentation of several of Gurdjieff's movements and dances are executed in spectacular fashion in that film. Also several of the more talented musicians in the Gurdjieff school, such as Laurence Rosenthal and Linda Spitz, have recorded the listening pieces and are available on CD for purchase.

Perhaps the most compelling recording, though, is that of Thomas de Hartmann, available on CDs that have been digitalized from often poorly recorded performances. Also available, though harder to obtain, are recordings of Gurdjieff himself playing his harmonium or hand-organ.

Meetings

Another essential condition created for the Gurdjieff pupils is the practice of regular meetings: weekly group meetings for those on the same level of understanding and usually monthly communal gatherings for the group as a whole.

During the weekly meetings students on roughly the same level of development are invited to bring their questions to elders for a response, or, for those who are sufficiently experienced, meetings with peers in which they exchange with one another on a collegial basis. The intention is not so much an exchange of conceptual concerns but, in concert with the direction of the teaching, an exchange of energetic influence, an influence that for each participant furthers their own journey into the unknown.

During the monthly – or, in some groups, weekly – gatherings all members of the group with sufficient experience are invited to participate in a collection of activities that serve to weaken the hold of the conceptual mind with its desire-driven concerns and identity and thereby strengthen the wish to submit to the higher mind and its motivationless interest in the moment. Such activities include participation in various crafts and the sharing of communal meals.

The sharing of meals, instituted by Gurdjieff, gives all participants an opportunity to share observations and once again ask questions, usually questions that concern those in the process of moving from an abiding interest in conceptual matters to a more fruitful interest in energy. Those elders who respond to such questions do so with a view not to reinforce the conditioning of the conceptual mind but to reorient the aspirant from concepts to energy, from a conceptual interest in being to a direct reception of Being itself.

Being and Becoming

As in other authentic spiritual schools, being and becoming work in tandem to actualize the spiritual potential of a given individual in a particular Gurdjieff house of work. This integral work provides an instructive example of how the conceptual mind cannot have direct access to the real.

Ever since the ancient Greek philosophers, the pre-Socratics, began to speculate about reality, being and becoming have been antithetical concepts. As such, they pointed mutely to only a partial recognition of the real, and the only way to transcend this apparent opposition was an extended period of study in a spiritual school such as Plato's Academy or, even earlier, the school of Pythagoras. There one could observe for oneself the mutually beneficial reciprocity of being and becoming and, eventually, recognize both as Being itself.

In this regard no other contemporary spiritual school matches the Gurdjieff school not only in providing access to this reciprocity but also in reminding a postmodern culture of the possibilities that lie beyond the conceptual mind. The decisive lesson to be learned is that the mutuality of being and becoming can only obtain in a school in which their reciprocity issues in a development of being from fragmentation to unity.

CHAPTER SIX

MODERN AND POSTMODERN PSYCHOLOGICAL THOUGHT

Goethe's Legacy

As we have seen in a previous chapter, Goethe was the source of an idea that has issued in an entirely different sort of science than the paradigm of physics and the other physical sciences: a poetic science that does not rely on mathematics as conventionally conceived and practiced. At the same time, the scientific protocols recommended by Goethe have much in common with the experimental sciences.

In opposition to the Western philosophical tradition of searching for essences and certain knowledge, Goethe advised the positing of working hypotheses based upon observations, and exposing these conjectures to empirical test – not, however, experimental testing as conducted in a scientific laboratory, but experiential testing conducted in a communal exchange of likeminded individuals. If a given hypothesis was to be fruitful, it needed to be vulnerable to possible falsification, or at least capable of being revised based upon ongoing examination of relevant evidence. In this way knowledge could be advanced without lapsing into doctrinaire speculation. In brief, Goethe's legacy insists upon a consideration of objections and alternatives, a weighing of evidence for or against a given hypothesis.

Nietzsche's Psychology of Masks

Nietzsche furthered Goethe's vision of a poetic science by developing his psychology of masks. The question of adopting a mask to hide one's true face, or playing a role, is a subtle one, and the popular notion that either donning a mask or playing a role is inauthentic and evil is an idea that Nietzsche vigorously disputed.

In agreement with the teaching of spiritual schools, Nietzsche wrote that most people already confuse themselves, their identities, with their roles, with their functioning in society, a phenomenon best understood in the favorable context of a spiritual school. For most individuals role playing does not exist in any meaningful sense: they simply *are* their roles – or rather, they are not, and if confronted with their confusion would admit they are not, but for most of their lives do not consciously see themselves apart from their roles. The quip about the M.D. or Medical Doctor degree – "Me Doctor" – is rooted in this insight about the identification of one's being with one's role. So what is inauthenticity in this context? Is it the playing of a role, or is it identifying one's being, one's sense and feeling of 'I', with the role? Surely it is the latter rather than the former.

So Nietzsche approves of conscious role playing, and associates it with being authentic, true to one's self, and for Nietzsche this deliberate donning of a mask is also congruent with intellectual honesty. "Whoever is profound loves masks," he wrote. In playing a role there is also a certain joy or delight, not a delight in deceiving others, but the joy of authentic being-in-the-world, to borrow some of Heidegger's translated language.

This notion of conscious role playing continues Goethe's interest in development and opposes what Nietzsche would call a "sick philosopher's" interest in the essence of a man or woman, what they "really are" apart from their deeds and works or creations. In this regard both Goethe and Nietzsche are more interested in the ancient Greek idea of artistic activity: that the Greeks knew how to experiment with themselves, create themselves, develop themselves through their artistic creations. As Nietzsche put it, "*They really became actors,*" that is, through conscious role playing, and through adopting different roles as experiments, they developed themselves. Without much anxiety about who they "really are," the ancient Greeks discovered themselves through their deeds and works. Neither Goethe nor Nietzsche, however, understood the mutual reciprocity of being and becoming or development that obtained in ancient spiritual schools.

Consciousness Is a Surface

"Consciousness is a surface," Nietzsche's own words, sum up his other extension of Goethe's legacy. Nietzsche argued that the importance of our usual or ordinary consciousness is widely overestimated, and that beneath this surface are hidden influences that decisively condition all we think, say, and do. And although Nietzsche did not understand how the mind works to create and sustain a false identity, he did appreciate how desires, many not understood or recognized, condition our most cherished beliefs about ourselves and our abilities.

In his psychology of world views, Nietzsche maintained that our most cherished beliefs about ourselves and the world are conditioned by parents, peers, and culture, are usually historically blind, absent of the need to consider objections and alternatives, and our reasons for believing are rationalizations. In this regard Nietzsche anticipated Freud, and indeed Freud admitted that Nietzsche "anticipated the laborious results of psycho-analysis" by his deliberate development of Goethe's legacy.

Freud's Legacy

With the advent of Freud's therapeutic psychology which included theories and methods the legacy of Goethe came to full fruition, in effect guaranteeing its lasting influence in Western culture. Freud's poetic science fulfilled Goethe's vision of a testable, nonmathematical science open to objections and alternatives.

The notion that Freud was a dogmatic tyrant bent on dominating his followers cannot withstand the available evidence, in particular the very interesting exchange of letters between Freud and his erstwhile disciple Jung. Freud is willing to consider objections and alternatives to his theories, including Jung's, but is not willing to alter them unless he is convinced that they need alteration. Freud did exhibit a willingness to alter his theoretical ideas later in his career, and also changed therapeutic modalities in light of practical experience with his patients.

Freud's basic therapeutic approach was a matter of remembering repressed emotional material, repeating them in the presence of the therapist, and then working through disowned matters with the therapist's help. Where Freud thought psychoanalysis could help best was in the first two steps; where he learned that therapy could not help was in the resolution of disowned material through "working through."

His theoretical outlook is best presented in his *Introductory Lectures*, but his later *Civilization and its Discontents* makes for better reading and offers a more comprehensive idea of his later thought. Like Nietzsche, Freud is a superb German prose stylist, and although his style suffers in translation it is still a marvel to read in English. The basic thesis of the latter book is that the instinctual drives or desires of the human being are in unresolvable conflict with the demands of civilization. The end result is that human beings are frustrated in their capacity to satisfy their desires, particularly the more instinctual sex and aggressive drives, and cannot expect to attain much in the way of happiness; indeed, Freud's rather bleak outlook prognosticates that what usually passes for "happiness" is a rather typical, and expected, unhappiness. Given the existential situation of men and women in civilized society, that is the best for which one can hope.

Whether one agrees with Freud or not, a correct assessment of his legacy is that more than any other major thinker he has advanced Goethe's vision of a poetic science. In so doing, he has also blazed a trail that many psychologists have followed, a trail that has widened into a superhighway.

C.G. Jung

Jung is by far the most interesting of Freud's followers, and was selected by Freud to be his gentile ambassador amid a host of Jewish disciples. Until, that is, Jung took what he considered to be a radically different approach to mental health and emotional distress.

Jung was intrigued by esoteric studies, and delved into areas which also interested Freud but which the latter man did not attempt to utilize in his psychology; however, Freud was influenced by the Jewish mystical tradition, as Bakan has shown in his *Sigmund Freud and the Jewish Mystical Tradition*. Much of this influence, though, was not something Freud either acknowledged or, most likely, about which he was even aware.

For Jung Freud's theory of libido as exclusively sexual was too narrow; instead, he thought of libido as a more generalized energy, much as the East conceived of *prana*, where Jung first borrowed the idea. Jung took interest in the study of yoga, traveled to India, lectured about *kundalini*, and counseled Westerners to avoid a serious immersion in Eastern practices and investigate the Western esoteric traditions instead. In concert with this advice, Jung turned to a study of Western alchemy, finding in its metallurgical symbolism a naïve, pre-critical – that is, pre-Kantian – presentation of psychological processes.

With the study of alchemy Jung was given a precious opportunity to entertain the possibility of an authentic transformational, sacred psychology in which higher energy played a predominant role; unfortunately, he was unable to consider this possibility and instead insisted that as a modern, empirical clinician he could read the symbolism of the alchemists in only one way: psychologically, and specifically in his own form of "analytical" psychology. Like his mentor Freud, Jung was able to travel only so far along the esoteric path to knowledge and being.

The Psychodynamic School

The psychodynamic practitioners of psychology, exemplified best by Freud and Jung, stress the dynamic processes of the psyche or mind in their writings and to a perhaps greater degree in their practice, but this is mostly lip service: lip service in the content of their thought and in the therapeutic setting as well.

The emphasis in their writings is *about* dynamic, energetic processes, not a pointing beyond the words *to* something real and discoverable; similarly, in the therapeutic setting more time is devoted to interpretation and other forms of "talk therapy" than to the discovery of energy, of Thought itself, beyond concepts or words. Thus the psychodynamic school of thought is largely theoretical and, in the spirit of Goethe, uninterested in the discovery of certainty, of being.

The Cognitive-Behavioral School

Another major school of psychology is what has become known as the cognitive-behavioral school. Major theorists include Albert Bandura and B.F. Skinner, and later cognitive theorists include Albert Ellis and Aaron Beck. Conceived primarily in academic circles, behavioral psychology entered the therapeutic arena as behavior modification, treating such maladies as phobias. Originally the contents of the mind were of no interest, but later the cognitive revolution changed all that, and behavioral practitioners began to see that cognitive interventions comported well with behavioral modalities.

What characterizes this school is its almost exclusive interest in the content of thought. Dysfunctional thoughts lead to dysfunctional behaviors, and in addition to strictly behavioral methods like desensitization therapists intervene by attempting to change the content of a client's thinking, encouraging functional thought and discouraging dysfunctional thought. Albert Ellis goes so far as to characterize functional thought as rational and dysfunctional thought as irrational.

Rationality, then, is conceived as a matter of thought-content, as well as the logical reasoning used to reach conclusions about oneself, others, and the world. Any suggestion that reason either could or should be used to know reality directly would be met either with indifference or, in the case of a practitioner like Ellis, outright disdain. Ellis admires the Stoic school of philosophy but has no use for their interest in the reality of being. What matters is their indifference to fate. What is not seen is that this "indifference" depends upon the mutual working of being and becoming.

The Third Force

The so-called third force or humanistic school of psychology has already been mentioned as a school that became interested in applying the sort of group work practiced in the Gurdjieff school to the helping profession of psychology, and that this school was less interested in the "sick" or "maladjusted" individual and more interested in the "self-actualized" individual.

Abraham Maslow formulated a hierarchy of needs, and atop this pyramid was the need to actualize one's potential. Toward the end of his career Maslow discussed what he called Being-needs or B-needs, coming very close to the formulations of spiritual schools in their understanding of the ontological need for Being. He also suggested that a more comprehensive psychology of the future must be "centered in the cosmos" rather than being centered in human concerns. Again, this formulation comes quite close to the ancient, sacred idea of man as a *potential* microcosmos. Thus the only "actualization" worthy of that name is the creation of a complete cosmos in men and women: a microcosmic reality.

The Transpersonal School

Maslow named this future psychology the fourth force, which came into being shortly after his death. It became known as the transpersonal school of psychology, with prominent clinicians like Roger Walsh and James Fadiman and the major theorist of the school, Ken Wilber. Wilber later renounced his association with this school and founded the Integral approach to life in general and psychology in particular.

Wilber's early thought set the agenda and tone of the school: just as a given human being tends to gravitate toward a particular level of development – say, the ego level – so a given therapist should target an intervention toward that level in order to address the concerns of that level and so facilitate movement to the next level. Wilber took conventional developmental studies by such researchers as Piaget and Loevinger and supplemented them with spiritual studies of development by Eastern thinkers like Aurobindo. Thus the transpersonal levels beyond the conventional levels were included in an approach that tried to account for psychological and spiritual growth or development beyond the accounts of other schools of modern psychology.

Postmodern Developments

Several decades elapsed, during which time the influence of Eastern spiritual teachings began to penetrate the Western psyche. Starting with an interest in Eastern thought among countercultural youth in the late 1960s, the first indications of a sea change was shortly thereafter with the aforementioned humanistic and transpersonal schools of psychology.

The 1980s saw a growing interest in "New Age" culture, including written works and music. During the 1970s and 1980s many entering professions related to psychology brought to their graduate studies an ongoing interest in Eastern thought, specifically the many remedial ideas and methods related to the process of desire. Noticing shortcomings in conventional psychological ideas and methods, they began to consider adapting these Eastern ideas and methods for use in helping others, analogous to the humanistic practitioners adapting group methods.

Specifically postmodern, Western ideas were also favored in the 1990s and in subsequent decades. The philosophy of Stephen Pepper, for example, was drawn upon in the cognitive-behavioral school in putting more emphasis upon a contextual approach to the question of identity. Practitioners in psychodynamic schools like Mark Epstein adapted methods from their personal spiritual practice, methods like mindfulness and a more radical form of self-inquiry than had previously been practiced. Epstein, for example, was convinced that the Freudian difficulty of working through disowned emotional material could be more fruitfully and effectively addressed by asking *who* it is having such difficulty; in this way the question of identity replaces the question of the resolution of past difficulties in importance, and is also seen as the solution to such difficulties.

From Resignation to Remedy

While some mental health practitioners remain stubbornly ensconced in Freud's resignation to an unhappy existence, the more innovative movement of Western psychological thought has been from resignation to remedy, principally as a result of the influence of Eastern upon Western thought.

Freud's rather bleak outlook regarding the prospect of using the rationality of the ordinary mind to effect substantial personality change parallels the resignation of the larger holding culture in the West about the ability of that rationality to know the real. In this regard Freud, in fulfilling Goethe's legacy, also bodies forth the limitations of that legacy: a lack of interest in being along with an exclusive interest in development or becoming. And it is precisely this lack of interest in being that decisively arrests the possibility of an authentic development – not of personality, but of being.

What Freud and other practitioners of modern psychotherapy overlooked was the mutual fecundation of being and becoming. The impediment to "working through," for example, arises because without help from a vertical influence there is insufficient being to effect a change along the horizontal dimension of human functioning. Freud's version of self-inquiry was not radical enough to attract help from above. So with a conventional sense of being, of identity, one cannot, even with therapeutic counsel, come to a resolution of unresolved material. What is needed for further therapeutic progress is an adaptation of methods originally intended for inner work in a spiritual school.

CHAPTER SEVEN

MODERN AND POSTMODERN RELIGIOUS THOUGHT

Religious Studies

Academic religious studies covers quite a span of topics, among them being biblical studies, comparative religion, theology, philosophy of religion, psychology of religion, mythological studies, to name a few. Fascinating as these topics are, their modern study tended to conform to the larger holding culture in the West, much as the Western psychological thought considered in the last chapter, until a similar sea change began occurring in the 1980s. Until then, modern religious studies was almost universally in agreement with the larger resignation regarding rationality.

We have already considered the fate of biblical studies, and how the pervasive skeptical outlook in that field at first disturbed more conservative religionists but later contributed to a kind of resignation about how much could be known about the formation, much less historicity, of the biblical text. Uncertainty about the Jesus of history led to a resigned reliance upon the Christ of faith, although even there any question about certainty was out of the question.

Philosophy of Religion

Philosophers of religion are by and large grouped in two camps: those who critique religious truths as being decisively false, and those who claim a special status for religious propositions. Both, however, agree that reason cannot know the truth directly, and that one must resign oneself either to believing or not believing religious statements. Such belief is called "faith."

The latest wrinkle in philosophy of religion is the so-called new atheism, although it is much like the old atheism of Antony Flew, Kai Nielsen, and Walter Kaufmann. In many respects it lacks the sophistication of the older attacks upon religious statements, and fails to take into account Wittgensteinian defenses of such propositions by philosophers like Norman Malcom. The latter sort of defense argues that religious statements are not like scientific statements, and hence serve a different purpose in the lives of those who are religious in thought and behavior. Yet once again, there is really no disagreement about the truth claims of religion: religious statements cannot deliver absolute certainty regarding the truth of anything; they can only confess belief or disbelief.

Philosophy of religion, then, joins the rest of the culture in a nihilistic shrug of resignation concerning what the reason of the ordinary mind can know. At best, religious statements are confessional.

Comparative Religion

A similar resignation obtains in the comparative study of religions. Scholars interested in this sort of study are not confessional at all; instead, they compare religions with one another along historical, theological, philosophical, psychological, sociological, mythical, and confessional lines. A given scholar, for example, might compare the three major monotheistic religions, Judaism, Christianity, and Islam, along theological lines of inquiry, but at no time does the question of which of these religions is true ever arise.

In brief, in the comparative study of religions reason is confined to comparison, not to the determination of truth. Although scholars engaged in such studies do not consider this approach a resignation of any kind, it nonetheless comports well with the larger resigned attitude to the reach of reason in the holding culture of the West.

Psychology of Religion

A wide ranging set of views obtains in the psychology of religion, from the dismissive position of Freud to the favorable position of William James, but in trying to account for why people are religious the question of whether religions are true is never seriously entertained. Once again reason is confined to less elevated concerns, the concern with truth being beyond the scope of psychology.

Even Jung, who was so taken with religious topics, psychologized religious concerns to such an extent that any metaphysical or ontological implications were dismissed as of no interest to a psychologist. Any overriding concern with truth was slighted by Jung as being pre-critical and naïve. Thus he could only characterize medieval alchemy, for example, as a stammering attempt to symbolize psychological processes of "individuation."

Theology

Although some modern theologians are confessional, the best are thoroughly Kantian in their approach. Paul Tillich furnishes the best example of an approach to theological thought that claims to highlight one's "ultimate concern" but in fact treats only penultimate concerns.

Tillich is an existentialist theologian insofar as he begins with existential questions; however, he quickly moves from such questions to what he calls theological answers, thus trivializing the questions themselves. Questions that so readily evoke "answers" are at best penultimate, and cannot be taken seriously. In his *Dynamics of Faith* Tillich maintains that "faith," or belief, struggles constantly and necessarily with doubt, and that this dynamic cannot be avoided. It forms part of his "courage to be," yet in this dynamic one cannot locate an authentic concern for being, for certainty; instead, one is yet again resigned to an ineffectual rationality that cannot disclose truth or direct development toward greater being and authentic faith.

Previous theologians like Luther and Calvin were explicitly confessional, but were also pre-critical by modern standards. Chastened by the Kantian critique, such theologies can no longer be accepted except as confessions of uncertainty. Kant thought he had made room for faith, but he only provided excuses for belief.

Postmodern Religious Studies

As the influence of Eastern thought continued its penetration of the Western psyche during the 1980s and beyond, more attention began to be paid to the Eastern religions with their remedial ideas and methods. By and large this newer level of interest did not change scholars grounded in modern resignation, but younger scholars appeared who recognized in remedial ideas a decisive alternative to Western resignation.

Two such scholars are Jacob Needleman and David Applebaum, both philosophers of religion. One of Needleman's first contributions was to introduce to a wide audience thinkers from the "traditionalist" school, itself a Western school of thought shaped by Eastern, primarily Sufi, sources, thinkers like Fritjhof Schuon, Rene Guenon, and Seyyed Hossein Nasr, in a volume of essays called *Gnosis*. These traditional yet also modern thinkers challenged the Kantian hegemony, teaching that the Intellect or *intellectus* can reveal the real.

Needleman's early essay "Why Philosophy Is Easy" contrasted the modern and postmodern study of philosophy in academia with the far more daunting study of philosophy conducted in ancient spiritual schools. In his *The Heart of Philosophy* he presents the aforementioned contrast of concepts with sacred ideas, and, while doing full justice to Kant's monumental achievements, questions the great philosopher's conclusions about our supposed inability to know the real.

David Appelbaum has written a short but important study of Kant's ideas, and in his other books, for example his study of Gabriel Marcel, *Contact and Attention*, he calls into question the regnant epistemology that has led to a weary resignation regarding what we can know. In place of the metaphor of sight, knowing at a distance, Appelbaum recommends the metaphor of touch or contact, knowing through immediate sensation.

Another scholar of note is the French historian of philosophy Pierre Hadot, who in his *What Is Ancient Philosophy?* highlighted the indispensable role of the spiritual school in the ancient quest for Being. Yet another French historian of religion, Antoine Faivre, has made substantial contributions to the advancement of our knowledge of esoteric Western spiritual currents of thought like alchemy.

A French scientist, Basarab Nicolescu, has written an important book on the esoteric thought of Jacob Boehme, who combined Lutheran thought with a Paracelsian philosophy of nature to produce what Pierre Deghaye called a theosophy.

Many other important thinkers could be listed, such as Joseph Campbell, Mircea Eliade, Robert McDermott, Gershom Scholem, Henry Corbin, and Ravi Ravindra. Campbell and Eliade were influenced to a great degree by Jung, but Jung's legacy did not prevent Eliade from making indispensable contributions in researches into yoga and alchemy, leaving open the possibility of a more authentic phenomenon in both studies than allowable by Jung and his more orthodox followers.

All of these scholars, although well educated in the regnant resignation of Western thought, were also well educated in the Eastern remedial traditions, and because of that were able to question in a serious way the conclusions of Western thinkers that appeared to bar the way to authentic knowledge and Being. Most agreed with Western conclusions about the inability of the reason of the disconnected mind to know the real; what they questioned was the pallor of resignation that hovered like a shroud over the Western mindset. Their suggestion was that given the varied remedies to this apparent impediment resignation was far from inevitable. It should at least be worth a try to take a few steps beyond the isolated intellect into a region that is admittedly unknown to the ordinary rationality. We will explore these suggestions in the final chapter.

CHAPTER EIGHT

———— ✦ ————

A LOOK FROM ABOVE

A Look That Is Free

> To live a more objective life would require an objective thought – a look from Above that is free, that can see. . . . My thought has the power to be free. But for this it must rid itself of all the associations that hold it captive, passive. It must cut the threads that bind it to the world of images, of forms. . . . This look from Above both situates me and liberates me. . . . my struggle is a struggle against the passivity of my ordinary thought, a struggle to let go of the illusion of my ordinary "I."

The author: Jeanne de Salzmann, Gurdjieff's designated leader of his school of work after his death, from her book *The Reality of Being*. In the section of the book from which this quotation is taken, Madame de Salzmann writes of the necessity to recognize a lack, a privation: the lack of an objective thought, the look from above that can see the subjective life of a human being with all its uncertainty and passivity, and in so seeing comprehend and understand it for the illusion that it is.

Not that we can rid ourselves of this subjectivity: we cannot, and by the "death of the ego" no authentic spiritual teaching means the complete removal of all subjective thought or feeling. Rather, the ego or ordinary sense and feeling of identity is seen objectively, from another level entirely – seen for the incomplete feeling of self that it is. For this we are called to live between two levels of Being, the lower and the higher. And this demands an inner development possible only in an organized school of work.

Discovery And Development

We have seen how difficult it is – indeed, how impossible – for ordinary thought to reconcile being and becoming, discovery and development. Yet this is what must be accomplished in order to attain an intermediate level of being, a level beyond that surveyed by modern developmental psychology and available only in a spiritual school.

Western thought was led to polarize being and development, so much so that its greatest thinkers were driven to embrace either one or the other: Kant embracing being or certainty, Goethe embracing development or becoming. Kant purchased certainty at the price of knowing reality, while Goethe championed development as the only reality worth knowing. Both were resigned to knowing only the contents of the mind, not the Mind itself, Being itself.

Eastern thought critiqued the mind's thought as thoroughly as did the West, yet without resignation; instead, the East offered varied remedies for the lack of authentic or objective thought, and although these remedies targeted different types of individuals they always called upon a higher level of Thought to supply the needed remedial help, always within the protected boundaries of a school.

Ancient Western schools also offered needed remedies, but because of the force of historical circumstance – in particular the development of Christianity as an historical religion that decisively shaped Western culture – Western thought was unable to retain the understanding of the indispensable need for an organized school of work as an essential countercultural requirement for the eventual upending of the illusions entertained by the holding culture.

The Passivity of Ordinary Thought

We have also observed how ordinary thought is in service to desire – not simply specific egoic desires, but the process of desire itself: identification of one's being with impulses intended to meet authentic need. And the images or concepts that represent forms of reality for us play an essential part of this enslavement or passivity.

Chief among these ideas is the constellation of ideas we hold about ourselves: who we are and what we can do. All such ideas have been deeply instilled in us, in the very tissues of the body, so much so that a threat to our physical form is a threat to our very being. What can challenge this embedded force? Only another force, a higher one, capable of penetrating the tissues of the body itself.

An Active Thought

A more active thought is not a disembodied "seeing"; rather, it is an embodied seeing, a higher force or energy penetrating into the body along the vertical axis of the physical form. This force alone can begin to loosen the thrall of the conditioned sense of self inculcated over a lifetime of cultural indoctrination.

In a previous chapter I wrote about what Gurdjieff called mind-observation, which is the initial sort of self-observation possible for new initiates in a spiritual school. Such observation, however, is not authentic self-observation, which is only possible within a state of being called Self-remembering. Self-remembering is *embodied* seeing, a look from above that penetrates into the body, particularly along the vertical axis of the back with deposits of energy collected in what Zen calls the hara, the abdomen.

Self-remembering is not something one can do; it is, however, a state of being for which one can prepare. One does not remember; one *is* remembered, remembered by a force from above. And as I have already written, only this force can liberate one from the force of a lifetime of conditioning.

Conceptual Conditioning

The conditioning with which we are enslaved is conceptual; it is comprised of concepts and continually reinforced with concepts. From earliest childhood we are subjected to a continual flow of concepts that decisively shapes our experience of the world and of ourselves. We are told that these concepts, and the rationality produced by them, reveals to us the only reality we can possibly know. That declaration is enough for most people; others, more inquisitive, are told, at least in the West, that centuries of serious thought has led to a kind of resignation about what we can know: the reality we can know is not really a direct revelation of what is, of Being, but is rather a conceptual representation of what is – that is the best we can do.

Some of the more inquisitive rest content with that conclusion; others, however, continue to search for other possibilities. This continued search usually leads one to a group of likeminded individuals, to a school of inner search for the real. And what one discovers is not just a teaching that points beyond the conceptual mind to a direct reception of reality but also entire traditions of similar teachings, all disputing the notion that reality can only be dimly apprehended by or rather through a conceptual net or veil.

The conceptual mind can be useful, however, in pointing beyond itself to what is. Sacred ideas intended to wean one from concepts and an altogether unworthy reliance upon the conceptual mind can be enough to initiate the all important transition from mind-content to Mind itself, Thought itself.

Intermediate Being

One such sacred idea is the notion of intermediate being, midway between the incomplete feeling of self conditioned into one and the higher, real Self or Identity. The attainment of intermediate being is a process of development, possible only in a school of organized work.

Another sacred idea is needed prior to a work toward intermediate being: the idea that we are fragmented. Our centers of intelligence or knowing are not connected, and our attention is too passive, not active enough to allow the needed connections to become established. Why has serious thought, East and West, come to see that the thought or reason of the disconnected intellect is not enough to disclose the real directly? Is it not because the other centers of intelligence or knowing are required for such a direct revelation?

Alone, the ordinary mind or intellect can only represent the real in images, forms, or concepts. Here we have the familiar sort of knowing, knowing at a distance, a subject knowing an object. Because of this distance, this separation, uncertainty obtains, and the conceptual mind is resigned to a knowing which is really not knowing. Only where there is no separation, no distance, can there be authentic knowledge. One can know only by *being* known.

Being Known

In order to *be* known – in order to be – one must be connected inside. The centers of knowing must be joined in a union made possible by a more active attention; this active attention begins with somatic sensation – a connection formed between the mind and the body. Two centers joined, the third center, the feeling, is called and cannot remain indifferent. And with the feeling of Being one is at last known and, being known, one can know reality directly.

The reality of being known cannot be easily expressed in words. One is invited to heed the call of Being, of being known, and of knowing authentically. Not as a subject knowing an object, two separate beings, but as one Being, inseparable, one Force or Energy, the Force underlying the apparent forms represented by our concepts. In submitting to this Force one begins the gradual transition from mind-content to Mind, from psychology to energy.

Transitioning from Psychology to Energy

Being known is authentic Self-remembering. And in *being* remembered one is initiated into an altogether new way of being, into an altogether new being. Our conditioning is conceptual, and in being conceptual it is also of course psychological. Ours is a psychological age, and such an age reinforces our psychological orientation at every turn. It is necessary to transition from a psychological to an energetic orientation if we are to know the real, if we are to be known.

This transition is not something we can do; however, it is something for which we can prepare. This transition is the major developmental task in the attainment of intermediate being. It is a development that can only be actualized by Being, by being known in the moment. Here we have the mutuality of being and becoming, of certainty and development. Being is required to develop, and development is required to receive Being. The resignation of the West is overcome in an immersion in a reality beyond the reach of the conceptual mind, in a synthesis of what Western thought had separated: a synthesis of being and becoming.

Reconciling Kant and Goethe

What so many Western minds have attempted to do, reconcile Kant and Goethe, being and becoming, cannot be accomplished with one center of intelligence alone – specifically, with the disconnected intellect. Yet once fragmentation is understood, this reconciliation occurs naturally as one submits to a Force from above.

Kant maintained that we must have certainty, at any price, and he was willing to urge upon us the price of not knowing the real. He thought he was making room for faith, but authentic faith is in fact the certainty beyond the ordinary conceptual mind which he insisted was impossible. Because we can only know reality as it appears to us, he thought, we can introduce faith as the weak tea of belief in scarcely believable doctrines, doctrines now made more presentable as ideas that can never be comprehended by reason. Contemporary Christians who maintain that their faith is rational have yet to understand the Kantian revolution in Western thought. If, however, the faith they proclaim is the certainty of Being beyond the ersatz reason of the ordinary mind, then it is indeed rational. By and large, though, their faith is the sort of "faith" written about by theologian Paul Tillich: belief vulnerable to doubt.

Goethe maintained that we discover ourselves through our development: what we do and the works we create. For this discovery, he thought, certainty was not only not needed but also irrelevant. We need no certainty about our identity or even about truth itself because the quest for absolute truth and knowledge is a chimera that distracts us from the more specific task before us: to create ourselves. As a disciple of Goethe, Nietzsche wrote about how we are called to give style to our character, and his ideal philosopher, the "philosopher of the future," would be an "artistic Socrates." Despite all his chatter about autonomy, Kant had no real feeling for autonomy and instead needed a bulwark of certainty or being as an anchor against the seas of change, of development. Nietzsche maintained that Goethe was the authentic model of autonomy rather than Kant, for the former created himself out of the courage to invite change and development.

Initiates of authentic spiritual schools eventually come to see how partial both these views are, how inadequately they represent reality even in words. And yet these two arguably greatest Western minds did share one insight: that the reason of the disconnected mind cannot fathom the real. And both shared the pervasive resignation that persists in Western thought to this day. Because Kant feared the uncertainty of change, he clung to certainty by proclaiming the essential categories of "pure reason"; because Goethe embraced this uncertainty, he found no value or interest in a quest for a certainty beyond any possibility of doubt, no interest in authentic faith. For Kant reason was confined to knowing how things appear to us; for Goethe reason was confined to the creation of ourselves. Neither could conceive of a reason beyond the reach of the conceptual mind.

Objective Reason

In attempting to address the question of an objective reason we come near to exhausting the capacity of language to convey meaning. The reason of the conceptual mind, the reason that both East and West have pronounced unable to know reality, is necessarily subjective. To use postmodern terms, it is perspectival.

The postmodern critique of the modern mindset in the West questions even more deeply the ability of the ordinary mind to attain any truth that is not embedded in already existing historical and cultural facts that decisively condition the search for truth and meaning. Each of us brings to the table our own unique perspective, our own subjective meanings, including our upbringing, our education, our unexamined assumptions, the very concepts that have been conditioned into us and by which we negotiate with consensus social reality. This postmodern critique makes any presumption of objective truth attainable by minds such as ours even more laughable. It seems, then, that objective truth, and the objective reason needed to disclose it, is forever closed to us.

And so it would be, if it were dependent upon the deliverances of our subjective minds. So far from being dependent upon subjective "truth," both objective reason and the objective truth disclosed by it demand the renunciation of all pretense to truth of any kind by the isolated, disconnected mind. The very idea that the disconnected, unsubmitted mind can attain any sort of truth must be decisively discredited if there is to be any possibility of a revelation of authentic truth or Being. For objective reason can only function in the complete absence of subjective reason, in a total surrender to the Force from above.

Subjective reason, along with the subjective "truth" disclosed by it, is conceptual. Within the protected boundaries of an authentic spiritual school this conceptual approach to the real must be questioned, pondered, and, finally, discarded as false and unfruitful – indeed, discarded as *the* impediment to objective truth. Objective reason is a feature of the whole being, while subjective reason is a function of only one part of a being, and a whole being is a mirror of Being itself, a "microcosmos," a small cosmos, not *reflecting* Being as the West has so often conceived the mind, but *being* Being. No separation, no distance, one Reality, one Force, one Energy. There is only Being, only Thought, only Reason. A Look, a Force, from Above.

A Science of Being

Objective truth is disclosed by objective science, a science of Being that Gurdjieff discovered and brought to contemporary culture in a form that such a culture, lopsidedly centered in the intellect, could absorb. Sacred ideas are presented to the intellect, ideas meant to wean one from that intellect.

Goethe's vision of a poetic science did not include the ancient study of mathematics as an intermediate stage of weaning one from concepts to a more direct apprehension of Being itself. He saw only the Newtonian usage of mathematics as a nonverbal account of theoretical ideas, a language that far from weaning one from the conceptual mind fettered one ever closer to it. Yet Goethe's vision is ultimately rooted in this ancient science of Being, though he was apparently unaware of it, partly because he failed to understand the necessity of Being to the intermediate development needed to transcend the ordinary social sense of self. His focus was upon self-creation as an indispensable ally to the creation of works of art. In this regard the creation of one's identity becomes analogous to outer creations.

Such an analogy only obtains insofar as a creative individual opens to the possible advent of a source of inspiration from above, the mysterious reception of the sort of insight or idea about which I wrote in a previous chapter. For the entire science of Being depends upon the blending of the higher with the lower to actualize the middle, the creation of an intermediate being capable of authentic action, and the creation of a material vehicle or subtle body capable of further, even finer receptivity and so creativity.

A science of Being is like other sciences in several respects. First an injunction is offered if the science is to be understood by an individual; in physics, for example, a certain amount of education is needed, to be followed by experience in conducting experiments. Without the acquisition of this information and experience one cannot understand the science. Second a way is offered to verify the ideas taught in the discipline: in the case of the science of Being, where direct knowledge is available, literal verification obtains; in the case of a science like physics, where only indirect and uncertain knowledge is available, either temporary confirmation or decisive falsification obtains. No direct verification is possible where no direct knowledge is possible.

The above considerations help to explain why an organized school is required in order first to learn and then to embody a science, in particular a science of Being.

The Liberation of Thought

Only a certain kind of thought can be liberated, because only that thought is enslaved: our ordinary, usual thought, in service to our passions, our desires, in turn subject to further thoughts, thoughts about who we are and what we can do. In brief, the culprit is a mistaken sense and feeling of identity.

An authentic science of Being, taught in an authentic spiritual school, challenges that mistaken sense and feeling. In so doing it also challenges all the sensations, feelings, and thoughts that orbit that mistaken sensation of self, in effect just about every sensation, feeling, and thought that a given individual has. Easy enough to see, given that all our psychological functioning is dedicated to defending and entertaining this mistake. So even though one's fundamental feeling of 'I' is directly disputed, all the psychology orbiting this feeling is also fair game in the quest to find the true and upend the false.

The purpose of the school's activities is twofold: first to upend the usual feeling of 'I', and second to introduce and instill the feeling of Being, the authentic feeling of 'I'. The development of an intermediate being is the growth of this feeling, the feeling of Being, a real feeling of Identity or Self. In upending the false and instilling the true, thought, ordinary thought, must itself be surrendered into a larger process of development; thought, the reason of the isolated intellect, must be surrendered into the advent of Objective Reason.

Ordinary thought is by and large a matter of talking to ourselves, what modern psychology calls self-talk. Cognitive approaches to better mental and emotional health advocate changing this talk, from negative to positive. Obviously positive talk beats negative hands down, but in a spiritual school all self-talk is challenged because such talk defends, entertains, and buttresses a mistaken identity. In order to upend this mistake all its manifestations must also be upended, decisively. Only in this way can a direct access to knowledge, to Being, to the truth, be made available.

Direct Knowing

Direct knowing is a function of the whole being, mind, body, and feeling. The sort of thought involved here needs no liberation: it is always and already free. The higher attention of the mind penetrates the body, revealing the always and already sensation of Presence in the body, a sensation and feeling *in* the body, not *of* the body, not the physical body, but the body of sensation.

Real knowing appears beyond concepts, words, or images, reveals reality without the conceptual mind. What appears is *what is*, reality itself, Being itself. Not beings, not objects known by supposed subjects, but just Being. Nondual, undivided, no separation, no division. Not even one, which implies two or more. Nondual.

A Thought beyond concepts, an Attention from Above. Awareness itself. Always already free.

Reconciling Intensity and Serenity

The ordinary, conceptual mind can never reconcile intensity and serenity; they appear to be opposites in every conceivable way, yet their reconciliation is effected in a direct experience or recognition of the real.

Intensity is almost always an immersion in extremity, and there are two ways in which this immersion can be experienced: one is the intensity in which an individual's parts are gathered into a more unified condition without an awareness of this change; the other is the intensity in which one is not only more unified but is also aware of the movement into a collected state of being. The first is the more common experience of intensity, although intensity itself is almost by definition uncommon; the second is a very rare experience, available only to those who have worked on themselves for some time. The first is just intense; the second is an intensity serenely comprehended or known.

Although intensity, as more commonly experienced, is an immersion in extreme situations, it can be serenely entered in a science of Being simply by understanding fragmentation and allowing a Force from above to unify one's disconnected parts. Existentialists make the mistake of thinking that intensity requires extremity. It does not. Intensity only requires a coming together of parts; it requires wholeness, the harbinger of greater being, the intermediate. And for this all that is required is a science of Being. The cultivation of vicarious or simulated extreme conditions of life is unnecessary.

If extremity were in fact essential to intensity, as existentialists suppose, then intensity would indeed be incongruent with serenity – not only in thought, but also in reality. Gurdjieff spoke of being present as "everything more vivid," which describes the experience of being both more engaged with life while simultaneously more removed from it. Like the concepts of intensity and serenity, the notions of engagement and removal appear opposites, yet in a collected state of being one is both more engaged and more removed or detached. One is both more intense and more serene than in usual, fragmented states.

Intensity I have already defined as the result of being more collected. I have yet to consider serenity. Serenity is the result of being loved, known, attended. One is bathed in love from above, as Jeanne de Salzmann has put it. Serenity is an energetic phenomenon, the Force or Energy of higher Being blending with the energies of lower being. And with that Energy come qualities unattainable by the lower: acceptance is energetical; nonjudgment is energetical; forgiveness is energetical; love is energetical; attention is energetical. All are features of serenity.

Serenity is like the sun, shining upon the saint and sinner alike. And in this blending of higher and lower, an intermediate, inner sun is created. Ascending from the wellspring, it radiates to eternity. One enters the marketplace with bliss-bestowing hands.

Objective Thought, always already available, awaits our attention.

The Enlightened State

Enlightenment, the enlightened state or ultimate state of consciousness, is supposed to be difficult to attain. The spiritual aspirant typically begins by seeking this state, and the metaphor of this search as a long and difficult journey reinforces this belief, the belief that Reality or enlightenment is a distant and formidable attainment. Yet according to spiritual masters, "It is only when you seek it that you lose. You cannot take hold of it, neither can you get rid of it." All other states – states of sleep and states of waking – can be entered and left; they have a beginning, and they have an end. The ultimate state, the enlightened state, Reality itself, Consciousness itself, is neither entered, nor left. Enlightenment cannot be attained because it always already is, and just as it cannot be attained, neither can it be shed or avoided. It is always already the case.

Whether physically awake, dreaming, or deeply asleep, whether spiritually asleep or awake, the enlightened state always is. It is the only permanent state, inclusive of all other states of being. It cannot be entered, nor can it be left. The enlightened state is actually the stateless state: it is Reality itself.

The Tibetan Buddhists speak of waking up as re-enlightenment, the recognition, the re-cognition, or knowing again, of an original and always already enlightened state of being. And it *is* a knowing again, a re-cognition, because since knowing and being are one, we already know, directly know, this eternal stateless state. It is the only state that never comes and goes, that abides always and everywhere; all other states, whether of physical or spiritual sleep or waking, have a beginning and an end; we enter such states and we leave them. But never, at any time, have we entered or left the ultimate state, the enlightened state, Reality itself.

Consider a brief exchange between Ramana Maharshi, a 20th century sage, and one of his devotees:

Devotee: How can I attain a state in which all impurities can be removed and the Self realized?

Ramana: You are in that state now.

Indeed, we are all in that state now. And being in that state, being that state, we know it, are always aware of it. Why, then, does it appear that we do not recognize, re-cognize, it? We are asleep to this recognition primarily because of the impediments we have discussed in this book: the process of desire, our mistaken identity, and the conceptual mind with its delusional thoughts.

The certainty we seek is the certainty of our own enlightened state. And in order to attain that certainty, a development of being is needed, an understanding of the misunderstandings that prevent that attainment. Enlightenment is not attained. Authentic Thought needs no liberation; it only needs our recognition. Liberation is not needed, for we were never bound. Ignorance is not; only knowledge is. Enlightenment is always already present.

That is the great discovery. Whatever lesser discoveries and subsequent developments have occurred before have all been leading to That, the discovery that we are, have always been, and always will be That.

And now, now that we have discovered That, what is the motivation for subsequent development? Is it to attain further being? No. It is sheer love of Being, a fatal attraction to That, fatal for what we once thought we were. A motiveless motive, rooted in wonder, a wonder that corresponds to the Reality that we are.

Development will occur because of this wonder, this love, but we will not be motivated by a desire to obtain something, to attain enlightenment, as we once were. Renouncing spiritual materialism, we court Being as we court a lover, not to obtain Her, to "attain" or possess Her; we already *are* Her. That is the great, the final renunciation. We renounce all attainment to re-cognize That.

What remains is the *what is*, the suchness, of every moment.

Coda

A cool breeze stirs the laurels,
As a distant bell tolls clearly through a crisp autumn twilight.
Through the evening mist a lone goose is flying;
Of one tone are wide waters and sky.

BIBLIOGRAPHY

Appelbaum, David. *The Vision of Kant*. Element. Rockport, 1995.

Be As You Are: The Teachings of Sri Ramana Maharshi, ed. David Godman. Arkana. London, 1985.

Bryant, Gary. *Invicti Solis: The Rise of the Unconquered Sun*. Balboa. Bloomington, 2015.

Burckhardt, Titus. *Alchemy*. Element. Longmead, 1987.

_____. *An Introduction to Sufism*. Thorsons. London, 1995.

Chogyam Trungpa. *Cutting Through Spiritual Materialism*. Shambhala. Boulder, 1973.

Coward, Harold. *Jung and Eastern Thought*. State University of New York. Albany, 1895.

Gurdjieff, G.I. *Beelzebub's Tales to His Grandson*. Penguin. New York, 1999.

_____. *Meetings with Remarkable Men*. Arkana. New York, 1985.

Hadot, Pierre. *What Is Ancient Philosophy?* Belknap. Cambridge, 2002.

Kaufmann, Walter. *Discovering the Mind*, V. II. McGraw-Hill. New York, 1980.

_____. *Existentialism from Dostoevsky to Sartre*. Meridian. New York, 1956.

_____. *Life at the Limits*. Reader's Digest. New York, 1978.

_____. *Tragedy and Philosophy*. Doubleday. Garden City, 1968.

Magee, Bryan. *The Philosophy of Schopenhauer*. Clarendon. Oxford, 1983.

Mead, G.R.S. *The Doctrine of the Subtle Body in the Western Tradition*. Solos. London, 1919.

Modern Esoteric Spirituality, ed. Antoine Faivre and Jacob Needleman. Crossroad. New York, 1992.

Muktananda, Swami. *I Am That*. Syda. South Fallsburg, 1978.

Nasr, Seyyed Hossein. *Knowledge and the Sacred*. State University of New York. Albany, 1989.

Needleman, Jacob. *The Heart of Philosophy*. Routledge. London, 1982.

_____. *What is God?* Penguin. New York, 2009.

Norbu, Namkhai. *Dzogchen: The Self-Perfected State*. Snow Lion. Ithaca, 1996.

_____. *The Mirror: Advice on the Presence of Awareness*. Barrytown. New York, 1996.

Ouspensky, P.D. *In Search of the Miraculous*. Harvest. New York, 1977.

Philokalia, ed. by St. Nikodimos and St. Makarios. Faber. London, 1986.

Ravindra, Ravi. *Yoga and the Teaching of Krishna*. Theosophical House. Adyar, 1998.

Real Philosophy, ed. by Jacob Needleman and David Appelbaum. Arkana. London, 1990.

Rorty, Richard. *Philosophy and the Mirror of Nature*. Princeton. Oxford, 2009.

Salzmann de, Jeanne. *The Reality of Being*. Shambhala. Boston, 2010.

Shaw, Fran. *The Next Attention*. Indications. New York, 2010.

Temple, Richard. *Icons and the Mystical Origins of Christianity*. Element. Longmead, 1990.

Waite, Dennis. *Back to the Truth: 5000 Years of Advaita*. Mantra. Washington, 2012.

Watts, Alan. *Myth and Ritual in Christianity*. Beacon. Boston, 1968.

ABOUT THE AUTHOR

Gary Bryant is an ordained priest in the Orthodox Catholic Church, a hospice chaplain, and a licensed master social worker. He has five master-level degrees, including theology, philosophy, English literature, business administration, and social work, having studied comparative religion at Rice University, the University of Chicago, and Harvard Divinity School. Gary is also the author of *Invicti Solis: The Rise of the Unconquered Sun*, published by Balboa Press in 2015.

With 30 years experience in a form of spirituality called the Gurdjieff Work, Gary is authorized by his own teacher to guide individuals and groups in that tradition. Gary is also past treasurer and president of the Prometheus Society, past membership officer of the Triple Nine Society, and a current member of the on line Four Sigma Society.

Printed in the United States
By Bookmasters